How to Choose a
Translation
for All Its Worth

Yet another book on translation? Yes, and this is the one I shall now recommend to concerned Christians who want to understand what the perpetual flap over Bible translation is all about. Few will agree with every judgment in its pages, but for courtesy to all sides, accuracy in technical matters, clarity of writing, a deep commitment to faithful rendering of the original, and an abundant supply of that least common gift, "common sense," this is the book on translation that deserves widest circulation.

—D. A. CARSON, research professor of New Testament
at Trinity Evangelical Divinity School

In his third *How to .... for All Its Worth* book, Gordon Fee has teamed up with Mark Strauss to produce another winner—*How to Choose a Translation for All Its Worth: A Guide to Understanding and Using Bible Versions.* It is a great read, filled with good illustrations from the numerous English translations from the past and the present, and written in an engaging way. Readers will be more accurately informed on how translation decisions are made and which translations are best suited for which audiences.... Fee and Strauss have upheld both *accuracy* and *meaning* while fairly evaluating the large number of English translations that have been given as a gift to the body of Christ.

—WALTER C. KAISER JR., president emeritus, Colman
M. Mockler distinguished professor of Old Testament,
Gordon-Conwell Theological Seminary

"Something gets lost in translation" is a common enough phrase, reflecting the difficulties of conveying what is said in one language in a very different one. With clarity and care Gordon Fee and Mark Strauss help us understand how translations of the Bible are done, what the difficulties are, and how the whole process is more of an art than a science. Moreover, they give us something of a history of English translations of the Bible, including a review of contemporary ones. This is the perfect little book to help the student of the Bible understand why different translations of the same verses look so different, and how to decide which Bible translation is right for the student in question.

—DR. BEN WITHERINGTON III, professor of New
Testament, Asbury Theological Seminary

This book, a must-read for pastors and Christians who love and read the Bible, is sensible (i.e., explains the why, what, and how of translation), sober (i.e., shows the strengths and weaknesses of all the major English versions), simple (i.e., in language a seventh grader can understand, and salted with illustrations), and spiritual (i.e., fills one with praise to God for the work of all translators and stops the unjust demonization of any translation).

—BRUCE WALTKE, professor of Old Testament, Reformed
Theological Seminary in Orlando, Florida; professor
emeritus of biblical studies, Regent College in Vancouver

There are so many translations out there—which one should we choose? Fee and Strauss do a marvelous job of explaining how translations come about, giving us the basis to make an intelligent decision. Everyone should read this book, but I particularly recommend it for seminary students, ministers, and anyone who teaches the Bible in schools and churches.

—TREMPER LONGMAN III, Robert H. Gundry
professor of biblical studies, Westmont College

Lay people often imagine that Bible translation is simply a matter of replacing one word in the original language with one word in the target language. Those involved in such work know that the matter is much more complex and that translation always involves interpretation. This work provides laypersons and specialists alike with a superb summary of the issues involved. Written in a style that is accessible to all, Fee and Strauss have cast theoretical and complex problems into everyday English. They have provided pastors and teachers who seek to guide their people through the translation maze with one of the finest resources available.

—DANIEL I. BLOCK, Gunther H. Knoedler professor
of Old Testament and PhD program coordinator,
biblical studies, Wheaton College Graduate School

One of the most common questions directed at biblical scholars is, "Which Bible translation is the best?" These scholars are then faced with the challenge of summarizing a complex issue in a brief response. With the publication of Fee and Strauss's work, the scholar may simply respond, "I would suggest that you read this book." *How to Choose a Translation for All Its Worth* is the most reliable guide available to understanding the process of Bible translation and choosing one that is appropriate.

—SCOTT DUVALL, professor of New Testament,
Ouachita Baptist University

Finally, a book that translates for the average person what is good about translation and how they work! It is a little like you can't tell the players without a scorecard. So here is a very helpful scorecard on what to look for in Bibles and why. In sum, well done, much needed, thanks.

— DARRELL BOCK, research professor of New
Testament studies, Dallas Theological Seminary

This book is crammed with material that's understandable, theologically sound, generationally balanced, and practical. I wish I had read one like it fifty years ago. It's a must not only for Christian pastors and teachers but for the everyday Bible reader who wants to be better equipped to understand God's Word. It's a classic!

— WARREN W. WIERSBE, author, former
pastor of The Moody Church

What a blessing to us all! That's what *How to Choose a Translation for All Its Worth* will be to Christians everywhere. Gordon Fee and Mark Strauss have written a masterpiece on a much-debated and important subject. This book is unbiased, thought-provoking, and even inspirational as it creates a fresh appetite for understanding God's Word.

— JIM CYMBALA, senior pastor,
The Brooklyn Tabernacle

Fee and Strauss each have strong careers relating to English Bible translation issues, which have prepared them to write this book. At a time when fairness in debates about English Bible translation has suffered, Fee and Strauss restore fairness, along with scholarly substance, as they discuss important qualities to consider when choosing a Bible version. One strength of their book is the large number of examples used to illustrate translation points.

— WAYNE LEMAN, translation consultant with Wycliffe
Bible translators; reviewer for the NET Bible, ISV
(International Standard Version), and other versions

This book is comprehensive, fair, and accessible. Particularly helpful are quick explanations of specific translations and a glossary of terms. This thorough and engaging book will be helpful to pastors, teachers, Bible students, and anyone serious about understanding and choosing among Bible translations.

— AMY SIMPSON, executive director, Leadership Media
Group, Christianity Today International

It seems like new Bibles come out every week, and the overload can be overwhelming. Gordon and Mark are wise and trustworthy guides!

—JOHN ORTBERG, pastor and author,
Menlo Park Presbyterian Church

If you are bewildered by the smorgasbord of Bible translations and alarmed by the debates raging over which translations are safe and which are not, this book is for you. Gordon Fee and Mark Strauss are wise guides who help us sort through the issues and teach us how to make informed choices about the version(s) we read. This is an invaluable tool for anyone seeking a better understanding of God's Word.

—CAROLYN CUSTIS JAMES, author of *The Gospel of Ruth: Loving God Enough to Break the Rules*

This book delivers exactly what its title promises. It is not a sales pitch for any particular translation. Rather, it's a crash course that helps people understand why Bible translations are different. It teaches a lot about Scripture itself, so it's interesting and enjoyable to read. I highly recommend it, especially to church elders and church staff.

—SARAH SUMNER, author of *Men and Women in the Church*

The complexities involved in Bible translation are seemingly endless. Here is an excellent guide through its complexities—clear, irenic, informative, and appreciative. I don't know of any book quite like this. It is a wonderfully attentive guided tour through the land of translations and their translations.

—EUGENE H. PETERSON, professor emeritus of
spiritual theology, Regent College, Vancouver

How to Choose a
Translation
for All Its Worth

A Guide to Understanding and Using Bible Versions

Gordon D. Fee
Mark L. Strauss

ZONDERVAN.com/
AUTHORTRACKER
follow your favorite authors

We want to hear from you. Please send your comments about this book to us in care of zreview@zondervan.com. Thank you.

ZONDERVAN

How to Choose a Translation for All Its Worth
Copyright © 2007 by Gordon D. Fee and Mark L. Strauss

Requests for information should be addressed to:

Zondervan, *Grand Rapids, Michigan 49530*

Library of Congress Cataloging-in-Publication Data

Fee, Gordon D.
    How to choose a translation for all its worth : a guide to understanding and using Bible versions / Gordon D. Fee and Mark L. Strauss.
      p. cm.
    Includes bibliographical references.
    ISBN: 978-0-310-27876-4
    1. Bible—Translating. 2. Bible—Versions. I. Strauss, Mark L. II. Title.
BS449.F44—2004
220.5—dc22
                                              2007026423

Interior design: Tracey Walker

Printed in the United States of America

HB 08.29.2017

For John H. Stek
friend and translator without peer

Contents

Abbreviations of English Bible Versions

ASV	American Standard Version
CEV	Contemporary English Version
ESV	English Standard Version
GNB	Good News Bible (another name for GNT)
GNT	Good News Translation (new name for TEV/GNB)
GW	God's Word
HCSB	Holman Christian Standard Bible
ICB	International Children's Bible
ISV	International Standard Version
JB	Jerusalem Bible
KJV	King James Version
LB	Living Bible
NAB	New American Bible
NASB	New American Standard Bible
NASU	NASB Update
NCV	New Century Version
NEB	New English Bible
NET	New English Translation
NIV	New International Version
NIrV	New International Reader's Version
NJB	New Jerusalem Bible
NKJV	New King James Version
NLT	New Living Translation
NRSV	New Revised Standard Version
REB	Revised English Bible
RSV	Revised Standard Version
RV	Revised Version
Tanakh	Jewish translation of the Hebrew Bible
TEV	Today's English Version (older name for GNT)
TNIV	Today's New International Version

Preface

This book was first suggested to me by the publisher and members of the Committee on Bible Translation as a measured response to recent controversies about translational theories on the one hand, and resulting translations based on these differing theories on the other. These matters are basically dealt with in chapter 2. Unfortunately, average readers of the Bible tend to choose their Bible on the basis of rhetoric, pure and simple, which they either believe or disbelieve.

While I was at first reluctant to interrupt another project to take this on, the opportunity to offer such a book as a companion to the first two "How to" books became attractive for several reasons. First, experience in the church has indicated that people know little about the what and why of Bible translations, so there is a tendency to make choices that are not especially discriminating. People "really like" one version or another but are often unable to articulate why. Thus, one of the aims of this book is to help the average layperson make an informed choice about which translation will become their basic Bible of use.

Second, occasionally I discover that people using a translation based on "functional equivalence" (see chap. 2 for this term) from time to time want to refer to one they consider more "literal" (= formal equivalent), in order to find out what the Bible really *says*. Similarly, those whose primary Bible is based on formal equivalence consult one based on functional equivalence to find out what the Bible really *means*! This needs probing.

A third reason is that as a longtime teacher of New Testament at both the undergraduate and graduate level, I sometimes had reason to say of a given translation that "the translators really got it wrong" at a given point. So when I was invited to join the Committee on Bible Translation, it was time for me "to put up or shut up." Moreover, I had by then become conscious that any public disapproval of the translation most of my students were using was not only in "bad form," but had the danger of disparaging the Bible itself. So joining the Committee became for me one of the great learning experiences of my life, not to mention a wonderful bonding with scholars from a variety of Protestant traditions who have become good friends.

Still another reason I found this project appealing was that some features of contemporary translations, although explained in the translators' preface, tend to remain a puzzle to the average reader. This is true, for example, of footnotes that offer an alternative reading, either with a simple "Or ..." or with the curious statement that "Some manuscripts read ..." Some people probably wonder which reading—the one in the text or the one in the footnote—is the real Bible. It occurred to me that the opportunity to explain both the nature and limitations of Bible translation could bring real benefits to the church.

But it also became clear to me, even before I started on this book, that I would need help—lots of help—because although I have served on the Committee since 1990, translation theory is in fact an area that I have *written on* very little (except for chap. 2 in *How to Read the Bible for All Its Worth*). But in this case I needed help less with regard to the Old Testament as such than with issues related to translation in general. So I turned to a younger colleague on the Committee on Bible Translation, Mark L. Strauss, professor of New Testament at Bethel Seminary San Diego, who has spent several years both speaking about and writing on this subject.

Besides bringing many years of expertise on these matters to the project, Mark also helped to keep me from writing a book only for my generation of Bible readers, while I helped him not to forget that my generation still exists! While we hope this collaboration proves useful throughout, for us it became noticeably beneficial in chapter 4, on the matter of idioms. Here in particular we became aware of the speed with which English changes.

Mark and I also owe a considerable debt to my wife, Maudine, who read through every chapter with great care and with an eye toward the reader without technical expertise. Her own years of teaching in public schools in the fifth and sixth grades also brought another level of understanding to the task that we greatly valued. We are also grateful to those who read and commented on the manuscript, including linguist and Bible translator Wayne Leman, biblical scholars Karen Jobes and Doug Moo, graduate student Aaron Sherwood, Jimmy Brown of Athletes in Action, and our Zondervan editors Katya Covrett and Verlyn Verbrugge.

The end result, it should be noted, is a truly joint product. Mark and I were each responsible for the first draft of our selected chapters, but we worked together on all of them to give them a degree of uniformity helpful to the reader. Our greatest concern has been to make a sometimes technical, not to mention complex, subject as accessible as possible to as large a readership as possible. Our goal is to help people *understand* the differences among the various English translations and so to *make an intelligent choice* regarding the primary Bible they use.

Finally, a word about the title. The publishers came up with the suggestion that it be another "How to Read" book, but the nature of the subject matter made that problematic. For some time, at the publishers' suggestion, we toyed with "How to Translate the Bible for All Its Worth." But good sense finally prevailed, since the book is not intended to help people translate for themselves, but to understand the nature of translation and what lies behind the translation(s) they use. So the present title was settled on as serving both goals: we want people to understand how their "favorite" Bible version was created and to have the facility to choose a translation (or translations) that will serve them best.

Our ultimate concern, it must be emphasized, is not the content of this book as such, but that people will become both better readers and better students of God's Word. We gladly dedicate this effort to our ultimate mentor in this exercise, John H. Stek, who was one of the original translators of the NIV and who for two decades chaired the Committee on Bible Translation (which produced both the NIV and TNIV) until his retirement in 2005. It is hard for us to imagine a Bible translator with more skill and sensitivity as to what good English is all about—English that is at once sensitive both to the divine nature of the biblical text and to what "works" with regard to the English language.

Gordon D. Fee
Lent 2007

Part 1

The Task of Translation

The Task of Translation

Chapter 1

The Need for Translation

Many years ago a much-admired teacher of Greek stood before her first-year Greek class. With uncharacteristic vigor, she held up her Greek New Testament and said forcefully, "*This* is the New Testament; everything else is a translation." While that statement itself needs some qualification (see chap. 8 below), the fact that it is still remembered fifty-plus years later by a student in that class says something about the impact that moment had in his own understanding of the Bible. For the first time, and as yet without the tools to do much about it, he was confronted both with the significance of the Greek New Testament and with the need for a careful rendering of the Greek into truly equivalent—and meaningful—English. And at that point in time he hadn't even attended his first Hebrew (or Aramaic) class!

Since the majority of people who read this book will not know the biblical languages, our aim is to help readers of the Bible to understand the *why*, the *what*, and the *how* of translating the Bible into English. It will be clear in the pages that follow (esp. chap. 2) that we think the best of all worlds is to be found in a translation that aims to be accurate regarding meaning, while using language that is normal English. Nonetheless, our goal is not to tell the reader which translation to use; in the end, that is a matter of personal choice. And while we think that everyone should have a primary translation of choice, we hope also, in light of the richness of available options, to encourage the frequent use of more than one translation as an enriching form of Bible study.

The *Why* of Bible Translation

The question of "why biblical translation" seems so self-evident that one might legitimately ask "why talk about *why*?" The first answer, of course, is the theological one. Along with the large number of believers who consider themselves evangelicals, the authors of this book share the conviction that the Bible is God's Word—his message to human beings. So why a book about translating Scripture into English? Precisely because we believe so strongly that Scripture is *God's Word*.

But we also believe that God in his grace has given us his Word in very real historical contexts, and in none of those contexts was English the language of divine communication. After all, when Scripture was first given, English did not yet exist as a language. The divine Word rather came to us primarily in two ancient languages—Hebrew (with some Aramaic) and Greek, primarily "Koine" Greek. The latter was not a grandiose language of the elite, but "common" Greek, the language of everyday life in the first-century Roman world.

Although modern Hebrew and Greek are descendants of these languages, the reality is that the languages spoken in ancient Israel and in the first Christian century are not the same languages spoken today. For contemporary Israelis and Greeks, reading the Bible in their original languages is like our reading the English of its early writers, such as the fourteenth-century Chaucer. We recognize many of the words, but many we do not, and the grammar is especially strange to our ears.

The third answer to "why do we need biblical translation" lies with a reality that might seem obvious to all, but which is often misunderstood. This is the reality that languages really do differ from one another—even cognate languages (i.e., "related" languages such as Spanish and Italian, or German and Dutch). The task of translation is to transfer the meaning of words and sentences from one language (the *original* or *source* language = the language of the text being translated) into meaningful words and sentences of a second language (known as the *receptor* or *target* language), which in our case is English. At issue ultimately is the need to be faithful to *both* languages—that is, to reproduce faithfully the meaning of the original text, but to do so with language that is comprehensible, clear, and natural.

As we will see, this means that a simple "word-for-word" transfer from one language to the other is inadequate. If someone were to translate the French phrase *petit déjeuner* into "word-for-word" English, they would say "little lunch"; but the phrase actually means "breakfast." Similarly, a *pomme de terre* in French is not an "apple of earth," as a literal translation would suggest, but a "potato." Since no one would think of translating word-for-word in these cases, neither should they imagine that one can simply put English words above the Hebrew words in the Old Testament or the Greek words in the New, and have anything that is meaningful in the receptor language. After all, the majority of words do not have "meaning" on their own, but only in the context of other words.

One might try in this case, as one of the authors has done regularly in introductory classes, to present the word "bear" to a group of students and ask them what it "means." In response one gets a large number of "meanings" for the word (large furry animal, to give birth, to carry, to endure, to put up with, etc.), but never the meaning that was actually in the mind of the professor. For he and his family were from the American west coast and were now living in New England. They had asked a service station attendant for directions to a high school gym in a neighboring town so they could watch their son play basketball. "Go down this (winding) street," we were told, "and when you come to the tree, *bear* right." Although context gave us a fairly good idea of what was intended by the word, this was a usage we had never before encountered.

In other words, knowing "words" is simply not enough; and anyone who uses an "interlinear Bible," where a corresponding English word sits above the Greek word, is by definition not using a translation, but is using a "crib" that can have some interesting—and, frankly, some unfortunate—results.

Thus the *why* of biblical translation is self-evident. The Bible is God's Word, given in human words at specific times in history. But the majority of English-speaking people do not know Hebrew or Greek. To read and understand the Bible they need the Hebrew, Aramaic, and Greek words and sentences of the Bible to be transferred into meaningful and equivalent English words and sentences.

The *What* of Bible Translation

The ultimate concern of translation is to put a Hebrew or Greek sentence into *meaningful English that is equivalent to its meaning in Hebrew or Greek*. That is, the goal of good translation is *English*, not *Greeklish* (or Biblish). Biblish results when the translator simply replaces Hebrew or Greek words with English ones, without sufficient concern for natural or idiomatic English. For example, the very literal American Standard Version (ASV) translates Jesus' words in Mark 4:30 as, "How shall we liken the kingdom of God? or in what parable shall we set it forth?" This is almost a word-for-word translation, but it is unnatural English. No normal English speaker would say, "In what parable shall we set it forth?" The TNIV translates, "What parable shall we use to describe it?" The formal structure of the Greek must be changed to reproduce normal, idiomatic English.

At issue, therefore, in a good translation is where one puts the emphasis: (1) on imitating as closely as possible the words and grammar of the Hebrew or Greek text, or (2) on producing idiomatic, natural-sounding English. Or is there some balance between these two? In the next chapter we will introduce technical terms for, and a fuller explanation of, these approaches to translation.

While we believe that there is a place for different translation theories or approaches, we think the best translation into English is one where the translators have tried to be truly faithful to both languages—the source language and the receptor language. In any case, the task of translating into English requires expertise in both languages, since the translator must first comprehend how the biblical text would have been understood by its original readers, and must then determine how best to communicate this message to those whose first language is English. At the same time, since English is now the most commonly known second language throughout the world, at issue also must be how well nonnative English speakers will be able to understand and use the translation. Some of the versions we will examine in this book were developed especially for remedial readers or those with limited English-language skills.

The *How* of Biblical Translation

The *how* question concerns the manner in which translators go about their task. Here several issues come to the fore. First, has the translation been done by a committee or by a single individual? While some translations by individuals have found a permanent place on our shelves (the Living Bible being a case in point), there is a kind of corrective that comes from work by a committee that tends to produce a better final product.

Second, if the translation was produced by a committee, what kind of representation did the committee have? Was there a broad enough diversity of denominational and theological backgrounds so that pet points of view seldom won the day? Did the committee have representation of both men and women? Was there a broad range of ages and life experiences? Did the committee have members who were recognized experts in each of the biblical languages and in the matters of textual criticism regarding the transmission of both the Hebrew and Greek Bible? Were there English stylists on the committee who could distinguish truly natural English from archaic language?

Third, if translation decisions were made by a committee, what was the process of deciding between competing points of view? Was the choice made by simple majority, or did it require something closer to a two-thirds or three-quarters majority in order to become part of the final version of the translation?

While the majority of readers of this book will not have easy access to the answers to these questions, most modern versions have a preface that gives some of the information needed. It is good to read these prefaces, so as to have a general idea of both the makeup of the committee and of the translational theory followed.

We should note at the end of this introductory chapter that in recent years there has emerged a great deal of debate over which of these kinds of translation has the greater value—or in some cases, which is more "faithful" to the inspired text. But "faithful" in this case is, as with "beauty," often in the eye of the beholder. While we are convinced that a translation based on "functional equivalence" is the best way to be fair to both the original and receptor languages, we are also aware that at issue ultimately is which version communicates God's eternal Word in language that is accessible to the majority of English-speaking people. In this regard, almost all of them do. But some do so for certain readers more adequately than others. Related to this is the need for the translation to "read well in church."

While the authors of this book think the greater overall value lies with a translation that attempts to be faithful both to the biblical languages and to English, our ultimate goal is not to convince others of this. Rather, we hope to help readers understand the *how* and the *what* that goes into any good translation of the Bible.

In the chapters that follow, we will take up the issues of the *what* and *how* of biblical translation, spelling out in more detail *why* and *how* certain kinds of translations differ from others. We will also indicate the benefits and limitations of each type of translation. We then offer examples of the kinds of issues that all translators must face in order to render into both accurate and understandable English something that was originally expressed in Hebrew or Greek.

Chapter 2

The Meaning and Task of Translation

There is a common perception among many Bible readers that the most accurate Bible translation is a "literal" one. By literal they usually mean one that is "word-for-word," that is, one that reproduces the *form* of the original Greek or Hebrew text as closely as possible. Yet anyone who has ever studied a foreign language soon learns that this is mistaken. Take, for example, the Spanish sentence, *¿Cómo se llama?* A literal (word-for-word) translation would be, "How yourself call?" Yet any first-year Spanish student knows that is a poor translation. The sentence means (in good idiomatic English) "What's your name?" The *form* must be changed to express the *meaning*.

Consider another example. The German sentence *Ich habe Hunger* means, literally, "I have hunger." Yet no English speaker would say this. They would say, "I'm hungry." Again, the form has to change to reproduce the meaning. These simple examples (and thousands could be added from any language) illustrate a fundamental principle of translation: *The goal of translation is to reproduce the meaning of the text, not the form*. The reason for this is that no two languages are the same in terms of word meanings, grammatical constructions, or idioms.

What is true for translation in general is true for Bible translation. Trying to reproduce the form of the biblical text frequently results in a distortion of its meaning. The Greek text of Matthew 1:18, translated literally, says that before her marriage to Joseph, Mary was discovered to be "having in belly" (*en gastri echousa*). This Greek idiom means she was "pregnant." Translating literally would make a text that was clear and natural to its original readers into one that is strange and obscure to English ears. Psalm 12:2, translated literally from the Hebrew, says that wicked people speak "with a heart and a heart" (or, as some "literal" versions render it, "with a double heart"). This Hebrew idiom means "deceitfully." Translating literally obscures the meaning for most readers. The form must be changed in order to reproduce the meaning.

Two Approaches to Translation: Form or Function?

Corresponding to this distinction between form and meaning are two basic approaches to translation, known by the technical terms *formal equivalence* and *functional equivalence*.

Formal Equivalence

Formal equivalence, also known as "literal" or "word-for-word" translation, seeks to retain the *form* of the Hebrew or Greek while producing basically understandable English. This goal is pursued for both words and grammar. Concerning words, formal equivalent versions try to use the same English word for a particular Greek or Hebrew word whenever possible (this is called *lexical concordance*). For example, formal equivalent versions like the NASU and NKJV seek to translate the Greek term *sarx* consistently with the English word "flesh." Complete lexical concordance is impossible, however, since Hebrew, Greek, and English words often have different ranges of meanings. Sometimes *sarx* does not mean "flesh," and even these concordant versions render it with other English words like "life" or "body."

Formal equivalence also seeks to reproduce the grammar or syntax of the original text as closely as possible (this is called *syntactic correspondence*). If the Greek or Hebrew text uses an infinitive, the English translation will use an infinitive. When the Greek or Hebrew has a prepositional phrase, so will the English. Again, this goal cannot be achieved perfectly, since some grammatical forms don't exist in English (like certain uses of the Greek genitive case or the Hebrew waw-consecutive), and others function differently from their English counterparts. Nonetheless, the goal of this translational theory is *formal* correspondence as much as possible.

Functional Equivalence

While formal equivalence follows the *form* of the original text, functional equivalence, also known as idiomatic or meaning-based translation, seeks to reproduce its *meaning* in good idiomatic (natural) English. *Functional equivalence* was originally called *dynamic equivalence*. Both terms were coined by Eugene Nida, a pioneer in linguistics and Bible translation. Advocates of functional equivalence stress that the translation should sound as clear and natural to the contemporary reader as the original text sounded to the original readers. Consider 2 Samuel 18:25, where King David inquires about a messenger arriving with news from a battle:

"If he is alone, there is news in his mouth." (NKJV, ESV)
"If he is alone, there are tidings in his mouth." (NRSV)
"If he is alone, he must have good news." (NIV, TNIV)

"If he is alone, he is bringing good news." (GNT, NCV)

The Hebrew idiom "news in his mouth," translated literally in the NKJV and the ESV, is awkward English. In fact, no native English speaker would ever use this expression. The NRSV is even worse, with the archaic "tidings in his mouth." What sounded natural to the original readers now sounds archaic and unnatural. The NIV, TNIV, and other idiomatic versions (cf. GNT, NCV) use more natural English to express the meaning of the Hebrew.

Consider also Matthew 5:2, where Jesus begins his Sermon on the Mount:

"Then He opened His mouth and taught them, saying" (NKJV)
"And he opened his mouth and taught them, saying" (ESV)
"and he began to teach them saying" (NIV, NCV)

The Greek idiom uses two phrases, *anoigō to stoma* ("open the mouth") + *didaskō* ("teach"), to express a single action. For the Greek reader opening the mouth and teaching were not two consecutive actions, but one act of speaking (see Acts 8:35; 10:34; Rev. 13:6). The functional equivalent versions (NIV, TNIV, NCV) recognize this idiom and so accurately render the Greek, "he began to teach them." The more literal NKJV and the ESV are understandable, but they miss the Greek idiom and so introduce an unnatural English expression.

In functional equivalent versions, words are translated according to their meaning in context rather than according to lexical concordance. For example, a functional equivalent version would translate *sarx* with different English terms ("human being," "body," "sinful nature," etc.) depending on its meaning in context. In Luke 3:6, literal versions render *sarx* as "flesh": "and all flesh shall see the salvation of God" (NASU, ESV, NKJV, NRSV). Since the meaning here is "people" or "humanity," functional equivalent versions render it this way:

"And all people will see God's salvation." (TNIV)
"and then all people will see the salvation sent from God." (NLT)
"And all mankind will see God's salvation." (NIV)
"and all humanity will see the salvation of God." (NET)
"and everyone will see the salvation of God." (HCSB)

This example illustrates a fundamental principle of functional equivalence: accuracy concerns the *meaning* of the text rather than its form. Although *sarx* is translated with four different words in these five versions (people, mankind, humanity, everyone), the meaning is the same. Accuracy in translation relates to equivalent meaning, not equivalent form.

All Bible versions lie on a spectrum between form and function. Below is a chart showing approximately where the most widely-used English versions lie.

Translation Spectrum

Formal Equivalent	Mediating	Functional Equivalent
NASB KJV RSV	NAB NIV JB NEB	GNT LB
NASU NKJV ESV NRSV	TNIV NJB REB	NLT CEV
Tanakh HCSB NET	GW	NCV The Message

Notice that in addition to formal and functional versions we have introduced a third category, *mediating*, which represents a middle ground between these two. Mediating versions like the TNIV, NIV, NAB, HCSB, and NET are sometimes more literal, sometimes more idiomatic, seeking to maintain a balance between form and function.

The Best Approach: Choosing a Bible

So which translation method is best? While the goal of literal translation—to preserve the original words of Scripture—is a noble one in theory, in practice it simply doesn't work. This is because Hebrew and Greek words, phrases, and idioms are very different from English words, phrases, and idioms.

Even translations that *claim* to be essentially literal constantly modify Hebrew and Greek forms to express the meaning of the text. Consider the Greek phrase that begins Mark's Gospel: *Archē tou euangeliou Iēsou Christou* (Mark 1:1). Most beginning Greek students would consider this to be simple Greek, which can be translated, "The beginning of the gospel of Jesus Christ" (NASU, ESV, NKJV, HCSB, NIV, NET). Yet even this is not a "literal" translation. The Greek grammatical forms are NOUN + GENITIVE PHRASE + GENITIVE PHRASE. The grammatical forms of the English translation are DEFINITE ARTICLE + NOUN + PREPOSITIONAL PHRASE + PREPOSITIONAL PHRASE. Almost all of the grammatical forms were changed to produce this supposedly "literal" translation. Furthermore, the phrase could have been translated, "The beginning of the good news about Jesus the Messiah" (TNIV). What seems at first to be a simple and direct translation is in fact an *interpretation* using different English forms to express the same meaning. This kind of interpretation occurs in almost every sentence in the Bible.

So while formal equivalent translators try to proceed with a *method* of formal equivalence (word-for-word replacement), their decisions are in fact determined by a *philosophy* of functional equivalence (change the form whenever necessary to retain the meaning). The problem is that by focusing first on form, the result is often "Biblish"—an awkward and obscure cross between Bible language (Hebrew and Greek idioms) and real English. No one speaking English in the real world would use an expression like "there is news in his mouth" or "he opened his mouth and taught them."

Such examples confirm that, in principle at least, a functional equivalent approach — one that focuses on meaning first — is superior to a formal equivalent, or "literal," approach. In this book we will defend the view that *the best translation is one that remains faithful to the original meaning of the text, but uses language that sounds as clear and natural to the modern reader as the Hebrew or Greek did to the original readers.* Another way to say this is that the best translation retains historical distance when it comes to history and culture (enabling the reader to enter the ancient world of the text), but eliminates that distance when it comes to language (using words and phrases that are clear and natural English). In subsequent chapters we will examine the many challenges of producing a translation that is *both* accurate *and* readable.

Although functional equivalence represents the best overall approach, there is great benefit in using more than one version. This is because no version can capture all of the meaning, and different versions capture different facets of meaning. It is especially helpful to use versions from across the translation spectrum: *formal, functional,* and *mediating.* A good mediating version (TNIV, NIV, NET, NAB, HCSB) is probably the best overall version for one's primary Bible, since it is clear and readable, but also retains important formal features of the text. The formal equivalent versions (NRSV, NASU, ESV, RSV) are helpful tools for detailed study, since they seek to retain the structure, idioms, verbal allusions, and ambiguities of the original text. Great benefit can also be gained from the functional equivalent versions (NLT, NCV, GNT, CEV, GW), since these use natural English and so provide fresh eyes on the text. They are particularly helpful for new Bible readers, who are unfamiliar with traditional Bible language.

We would add, however, that idiomatic versions can be even more helpful for those who have spent their whole life reading and memorizing Scripture, since there is a tendency to become so comfortable with traditional Bible language — Biblish or "Bible-ese" — that they no longer consider carefully what the words actually mean. For example, in the second line of the Lord's Prayer all of the formal equivalent versions use the traditional "hallowed be your name." Consider how these functional equivalent versions render it:

"may your name be honored." (NLT)
"May your holy name be honored." (GNT)
"help us to honor your name." (CEV)

Functional equivalent versions encourage readers to move beyond traditional words and phrases and to consider carefully the meaning of the text. We must always remember that the Bible is God's *Word*—his message to us. And a message is of no use unless it is actually understood. All translation should be *meaningful* translation.

The recognition that a translation must ultimately focus on meaning over form is nothing new, and translators throughout history have grappled with this issue. The original preface to the King James Version of 1611 discusses the question of whether one English word should be chosen for each Greek or Hebrew word. The translators noted: "We have not tied ourselves to a uniformity of phrasing, or to an identity of words, as some peradventure would wish that we had done ... For is the kingdom of God become words or syllables?" These translators, who produced the most enduring English version of all time, recognized that the message of the kingdom of God was more than just words on a page; it was the meaning those words conveyed.

Martin Luther, the great Protestant reformer, translated the Bible into his vernacular German. In reflecting on the process of translating the Old Testament, he wrote:

> I must let the literal words go and try to learn how the German says that which the Hebrew expresses ... Whoever would speak German must not use Hebrew style. Rather he must see to it—once he understands the Hebrew author—that he concentrates on the sense of the text, asking himself, "Pray tell, what do the Germans say in such a situation?" ... Let him drop the Hebrew words and express the meaning freely in the best German he knows.[1]

Martin Luther understood that translation was not just about *replacing words*, but about *reproducing meaning*.

All Translation Is Interpretation

If the goal of translation is to reproduce the meaning of the text, then it follows that all translation involves interpretation. Some people say, "Just tell me what the Bible says, not what it means." The problem with this is that "what the Bible says" is in Hebrew and Greek, and there is seldom a one-to-one correspondence between English and these languages. Before we can translate a single word, we must interpret its meaning in context. Of course it is even more complicated than that, since words get their meaning in dynamic relationship with other words. Every phrase, clause, and idiom must be interpreted in context before it can be translated accurately into English.

Translation is, therefore, always a two-step process: (1) Translators must first interpret the meaning of the text in its original context. Context here means not only the surrounding words and phrases, but also the genre (literary form) of the document, the life situation of the author and the original readers, and the assumptions that these authors and readers would have brought to the text. (2) Once the text is accurately understood, the translator must ask, How is this meaning best conveyed in the receptor language? What words, phrases, and idioms most accurately reproduce the author's message? Translation is more than a simple replacement of words.

Since all translation involves interpretation, it follows that no translation is perfect. There will always be different interpretations of certain words and phrases, and no Bible version will always get it right. Furthermore, differences between languages mean that every translation represents an approximation of the original meaning. We have a saying in English, "Something was lost in the translation," and this is certainly true. Something, however subtle, is regularly lost in translation because no two languages are identical.

Throughout history this inability to translate perfectly has been recognized by translators—often with fear and trembling. An old Italian proverb says, *Traduttore traditore*, meaning "The translator is a traitor!" Although this play on words is certainly an exaggeration, it contains a measure of truth. Every translation "betrays" the original text because it is impossible to communicate all of the meaning with perfect clarity. A Jewish proverb says essentially the same thing. Rabbi Judah is reported to have said, "If one translates a verse literally, he is a liar; if he adds thereto, he is a blasphemer, and a slanderer" (*b. Kiddushin* 49a). You can hear the translator's frustration. Literal translation can distort the meaning of the text, but idiomatic translation risks introducing the wrong meaning!

Yet Bible readers must not despair. Although meaning can never be reproduced *perfectly*, it can be rendered *truly*, that is, with a high degree of accuracy. What Bible readers need to take from this is that all Bible versions—no matter how accurate—have certain limitations. These can be overcome by (1) using more than one version to gain a better perspective; (2) reading larger units of text to determine the greater context and flow of thought; (3) checking good commentaries on difficult passages; and (4) gaining a better knowledge of the world of the Bible through studies of its background and culture.

Students of God's Word have a wealth of resources available today that help to clarify the meaning of the text—more than at any time in history. We also believe in the doctrine of the "perspicuity of Scripture." This means that God has revealed himself clearly through his Word and it will be understandable to those who are willing to take the time to read and study it carefully with their hearts and their minds.

Isn't That Just a "Paraphrase"?

A comment should be made here about the word "paraphrase," since it is one of the most misunderstood and misused words with reference to Bible translation. The term is often used in a derogatory sense of a translation that is highly idiomatic and so (by implication) misses the meaning of the original. People will say, "Isn't that just a paraphrase?" and mean "That is not a *real* translation—it's too free." The problem with this definition is that it starts with the incorrect assumption that an accurate translation is necessarily a literal one, and thus an idiomatic one is inaccurate.

As we have seen, however, the opposite can be true. "What is your name?" is an idiomatic translation of *¿Cómo se llama?* but it is also accurate. "How yourself call?" is a literal translation, but it is inaccurate. An accurate translation is one that reproduces the *meaning* of the text, regardless of whether it follows the *form*. This realization makes the popular definition of "paraphrase" subjective and unhelpful. It would be better to use the term in a neutral sense, meaning "to say the same thing in different words, usually for the sake of clarification or simplification." By this definition *all translations* paraphrase to one degree or another, since all change Hebrew and Greek words into English ones to make the text understandable. The important question then becomes not whether the text paraphrases, but whether it gets the meaning right.

We should also note that linguists sometimes use "paraphrase" in a third sense, contrasting it with "translation." While "translation" is transferring a message *from one language to another*, paraphrase is rewording a message in the *same language*. By this definition, The Living Bible is a true paraphrase, since Kenneth Taylor started with an English version (the American Standard Version) and reworded and simplified it. Other functional equivalent versions would be true translations, since they were rendered not from an English version but directly from the Hebrew and Greek.

Original Meaning and Contemporary Relevance

Closely related to the question of form versus meaning is that of *original meaning* versus *contemporary relevance*. We have referred already to the issue of historical distance. The Bible was written not only in different languages from ours, but in a different time and place. All versions seek to cross the bridge of time and make the message understandable to modern readers. Some place greater stress on the original meaning, others on the contemporary relevance.

On the "Translation Spectrum" chart above (p. 28), we placed The Message, an engaging version produced by Eugene Peterson, on the far right side. This version is certainly idiomatic since it freely changes the form of the original text. But there is another factor at work here: whether a translation places greater emphasis on the original meaning or its contemporary significance. The Message has been called "a 'translation of tone' ... bridging the gap between the original languages and English, and between centuries of time and language change, to bring to us the New Testament as it originally sounded."[2] In other words, The Message intentionally eliminates historical distance not only with reference to language but also with reference to time and culture.

For example, in Matthew 23:27 Jesus accuses the Pharisees of being "whitewashed tombs, which look beautiful on the outside but on the inside are full of the bones of the dead" (TNIV). Both formal and functional equivalent versions refer here to "whitewashed tombs" or something similar (NLT, CEV, GNT, GW, NCV, etc.). But in The Message Jesus says to the Pharisees, "You're like manicured grave plots, grass clipped and the flowers bright, but six feet down it's all rotting bones and worm-eaten flesh." A modern cemetery, rather than a first-century rock-hewn tomb, is now in view.

This goes beyond translation to *transculturation*. While the goal of translation is to carry the modern reader back to the world of the text, transculturation brings the text to the modern reader, contemporizing it for today. The goal is less about original meaning and more about contemporary relevance. Like functional equivalent versions, The Message seeks to use clear and idiomatic English. But it goes beyond functional equivalence, whose primary goal is equivalent *meaning*, by seeking to provoke in modern readers an equivalent *response*. Peterson's intent was to recapture the tone, to bring out the subtleties and nuances of the Hebrew and Greek languages while keeping a sense of firsthand experience for contemporary readers. Peterson often asked himself, "If Paul were the pastor of my church, how would he say this?" or "If Jesus were here teaching, what would it sound like?" Notice that the question is not, "What was Jesus' message to his first-century readers?" but rather, "If Jesus were here teaching, what would it sound like?"

Other versions have done something similar. Kenneth Taylor's Living Bible often contemporized, changing "lamps" to "flashlights" (Ps. 119:105 LB) and the "holy kiss" to "handshake of Christian love" (1 Peter 5:14 LB). These renderings miss the original cultural meaning but make the text more relevant in the modern world. A much more radical example is Clarence Jordan's *Cotton Patch Version*, which rewrites the story of Jesus, setting it in the American South during the Civil Rights Movement. Jesus is born in Gainesville, Georgia, and lynched in Atlanta by the state governor and his religious cronies. Paul's letter to the Romans is now written to Washington, D.C., and Ephesians to Birmingham, Alabama!

More recent examples of transculturation include *Black Bible Chronicles* by P. K. McCary (1993) and Rob Lacey's *The Word on the Street* (2003). Both of these, in different ways, seek to transfer the message of the Bible into the language of the inner city. In doing so, they are willing to sacrifice the original context and culture of the Bible to sound fresh and relevant.

Just as all Bible versions lie on a spectrum between form and function, so all also lie on a spectrum between original meaning and contemporary relevance. Even the most literal versions at times contemporize the message to make it understandable for today's readers. For example, all of the formal equivalent versions on the chart above (except the KJV) read in Luke 24:13 that Emmaus was "seven miles" from Jerusalem, even though the Greek says that the town was "sixty *stadia*" away (a *stadium* was about six hundred feet). These versions have contemporized here and elsewhere by converting a Greek measurement into an English one. In chapter 6 we will examine the challenges of translating things that are unique to a particular time or culture.

The Goals of Formal, Functional, and Mediating Versions

One way to categorize the difference between the translation philosophies discussed above is to ask how far translators are willing to go in modifying the form of the Hebrew or Greek to communicate the meaning. As we have seen, all translations—even the most literal—alter Greek and Hebrew *forms* in order to communicate meaning. So what's the difference?

The answer seems to be that different philosophies of translation have different goals in mind. *Formal equivalent* versions seek to modify Hebrew and Greek forms until the text is *comprehensible*. *Mediating* versions modify forms until the text is *clear*. *Functional equivalent* (or idiomatic) versions modify the form until the text is *natural*. The following chart illustrates this, adding various strengths and weaknesses of each translation type.

	Formal Equivalence (literal)	Mediating	Functional Equivalence (idiomatic)
Goal	**Comprehension:** Alter the form until the text is *comprehensible*.	**Clarity:** Alter the form until the text is *clear*.	**Naturalness:** Alter the form until the text is *natural*.
Examples	KJV, NKJV, NASU, NRSV, RSV, ESV	NIV, TNIV, NAB, NJB, HCSB, NET	NLT, NCV, GNT, GW, GNT, CEV
Strengths	Helps to capture metaphors, verbal allusions, and ambiguities.	Achieves both accuracy and clarity.	Greatest comprehension. Communicates the message clearly and naturally.
Weaknesses	Can result in awkward English, obscurity, and inaccuracy. Comprehension test often fails.	More interpretation, so greater margin for interpretive error. Sometimes uses unnatural English.	Even more interpretation, so greater margin for error. Sometimes loses nuances of meaning in pursuit of simplicity and clarity.

Translation and the Doctrine of Inspiration

One of the surprising, and from our perspective unfortunate, recent developments in the story of English translations is the reappearance of an old argument that "literal" versions are more compatible with the doctrine of the verbal inspiration of Scripture. We say "old," because this is precisely what drove Robert Young (best known for his analytical concordance to the KJV) to produce a version vis-à-vis the KJV (first ed. 1862). In keeping with the historic expression of that doctrine, Young argued: "This inspiration extends only to the original text, *as it came from the pens of the writers*, not to any translation ever made by man, however aged, venerable, or good; and only in so far as any of these adhere to the original" (italics original). With this we would agree. But then he added, "neither adding to nor omitting from it one particle," by which he meant that

> if a translation gives a *present tense* when the original gives a *past*, or a *past* when it has a *present* ... an *a* for a *the*, or a *the* for an *a*, an *imperative* for a *subjunctive*, or a *subjunctive* for an *imperative*; a verb for a noun, or a noun for a verb, it is clear that verbal inspiration is as much overlooked as if it had not existed. THE WORD OF GOD IS MADE VOID BY THE TRADITIONS OF MEN. A *strictly literal* rendering may not be so pleasant to the ear as one where the *apparent sense* is chiefly aimed at, yet it is not *euphony* but *truth* that ought to be sought, and where in such a version as the one commonly in use in this country [the KJV!], there are scarcely *two consecutive verses* where there is not some departure from the original such as those indicated ... it is difficult to see how verbal inspiration can be of the least practical use to those who depend upon that version alone.[3]

His own "translation" of a randomly selected verse (2 Sam. 19:38) reads: "With me doth Chimham go over, and I do to him that which *is* good in thine eyes, yea, all that thou dost fix on me I do to thee." While this is surely "literal" gone off kilter, few readers today would say it is also "accurate."

Our first point, then, is that, as with beauty, "literal" is in the eye of the beholder, in this case meaning "in the perception of the user." This is why we have tried to avoid the word "literal" in this book and have often put it in quote marks when we use it—because those who use it tend to have such a wide range of meanings. Unfortunately, it is also often used in the literature simply as a rhetorical device over against "meaning-based" versions.

Second, much of this rhetoric represents a poor understanding of the doctrine of verbal inspiration, which historically does not refer to the words as "words in themselves," but "words as they convey meaning." It is precisely at this point that we would argue that a translation that places the priority of *meaning* over *form* is much more in keeping with the doctrine of inspiration, since at issue always is the "meaning" of the inspired words. The translation that best conveys that meaning is the most faithful to this historic doctrine.

A comparison between the doctrine of sacred Scripture in Christianity and Islam might be helpful here. The Muslim view of divine inspiration limits Allah's revelation to the *Arabic words* of the Koran. Translations of the Koran into other languages are not inspired scripture; they are "commentary." This is why we hear Muslim children reciting the Koran in Arabic, even when they do not know Arabic and have no idea what it means.

But that is not the Christian doctrine of divine inspiration, which concerns not words in isolation, but the *meaning* of those words in context. When lecturing on Bible translation, one of the authors often holds up an English Bible and asks the audience, "Is this God's Word?" The answer is a resounding "Yes!" This is absolutely true. An English translation remains God's Word when it faithfully reproduces the meaning of the text. And since languages differ in terms of word meanings, grammatical constructions, and idioms, translation can never be about simply replacing words. The Hebrew and Greek text must first be interpreted—word-by-word, phrase-by-phrase, clause-by-clause—to determine the original meaning. Then this meaning must be painstakingly reproduced using *different* words, phrases, and clauses in English. The translation that most closely adheres to the verbal and plenary inspiration of Scripture is the one that reproduces *the total meaning* of the text, not just its words.

Standards of Excellence in Translation

Having examined the nature of Bible translation, we can summarize four key criteria for excellence in translation. The best translation should be *accurate, clear, natural,* and *audience-appropriate.* As we will see, these criteria can sometimes be in tension, and no single version will always accomplish them all.

Accurate

By accurate we mean that a translation reflects the meaning of the original text as closely as possible. It should transport modern readers back to the world of the Bible, enabling them to hear the message as the original readers heard it.

Although accuracy relates primarily to properly transferring the linguistic meaning of the forms of the biblical languages, it also relates to biblical history and culture. Every book in the Bible was written at a particular place and time, and a translation should seek to reproduce the foreignness of the text.

Readers of the Gospels, for example, should experience the world of Jesus and first-century Judaism. In Matthew 23:5 Jesus criticizes the Pharisees because "everything they do is done for people to see: They make their phylacteries wide and the tassels on their garments long" (TNIV). Phylacteries were small boxes with Scripture verses inside, which pious Jews wore on their foreheads and arms to literally obey Deuteronomy 6:8; 11:18. Tassels on robes are commanded in Numbers 15:38–39 and Deuteronomy 22:12. These things were an important part of first-century Jewish religious life, so a good translation will seek to retain them.

Functional equivalent versions often provide explanatory phrases for this verse. The NLT reads, "Everything they do is for show. On their arms they wear extra wide prayer boxes with Scripture verses inside, and they wear robes with extra long tassels" (cf. GNT, CEV, NCV). The historical meaning is retained, but an explanatory phrase is used instead of the less commonly known technical term "phylacteries." The Message, however, intentionally avoids the cultural meaning by translating, "Their lives are perpetual fashion shows, embroidered prayer shawls one day and flowery prayers the next." This rendering creates vivid relevance, but at the expense of historical accuracy.

Accuracy also relates to genre or literary form. The translation of a New Testament epistle should read like a first-century letter, and an Old Testament narrative should read like an ancient story. Perhaps the greatest challenge here concerns Old Testament poetry, since poetry works not only through the meaning of words and phrases, but also through its aesthetic qualities. It is often difficult or impossible to preserve a wordplay in Hebrew or Greek or to duplicate the rhythm of a poetic section. We will discuss the challenges of translating poetry in a later chapter.

Reproducing the style of the original is also part of accuracy. A text written in a higher register or more formal literary style in Hebrew or Greek should be translated into a more formal English style. ("Register" here refers to the type of language used in a particular social situation or when communicating with a particular set of people. Language with a "higher register" is directed toward those with a larger vocabulary and greater competence in that language.) Similarly, a more colloquial or conversational style of Hebrew or Greek should be rendered that way in English. Mark's Gospel is fairly rough Semitic (Jewish style) Greek, while Luke's Gospel is a more formal Hellenistic literary style. As much as possible, a translation should reflect these differences.

One important clarification is necessary here. Register, or reading level, is not the same as translation philosophy. In other words, a translation done at a high register is not necessarily a literal one. Great works of English literature may be written at a very high register, that is, with complex vocabulary and sentence structure, but they do not sound like literal translations. Translations done at a high register should still sound like *English*, not Biblish, but they are free to draw more deeply from the rich resources of English vocabulary, style, and idiom. Mediating versions, like the NET Bible, TNIV, NJB, NAB, and REB, tend to be translated at a higher register than their functional equivalent counterparts.

Clear

A second important criterion for excellence in translation is *clarity*. While a Bible translation should transport the reader to a different time and place, it should do so with language that is clear and understandable. Obscure and awkward language may remind students that they are reading a "foreign" text, but it also moves the reader further from the original intent of the author, compromising the accuracy of the translation. This is because the original (in most cases) sounded clear and natural to the original readers. The exception to this is when a text is intentionally ambiguous, in which case the translation should seek to retain the same measure of ambiguity as the original.

Clarity can be compromised by consistently translating a Hebrew or Greek form with the same English form. One of the most problematic of these is the Greek genitive case. Beginning Greek students are often told to translate the genitive with the preposition "of," as in the phrase "the word *of God*" (*ho logos tou theou*). Here *tou theou* ("of God") is a genitive construction. The problem is that while many genitive constructions in the New Testament can be translated with "of + NOUN," others cannot. Consider these translations of genitive constructions (in italics) in formal equivalent versions:

"you were sealed with the Holy Spirit *of promise*." (Eph. 1:13 NKJV)
"he [Christ] upholds the universe by the word *of his power*." (Heb. 1:3 ESV)
"I pray ... that you will know what is the hope *of His calling*." (Eph. 1:18 NASU)

While in many cases the preposition "of" is a perfectly acceptable translation, in these examples it results in an obscure or misleading translation. What, for example, does "the Holy Spirit of promise" mean? The meaning of this phrase is the Holy Spirit *who was promised*, or "the promised Holy Spirit" (TNIV, NIV, NET, HCSB, NAB, ESV). We have here what grammarians refer to as an attributive genitive. Similarly, in Hebrews 1:3 the ESV's "word of his power" is nonsensical (word that his power possesses?). This is another attributive genitive, meaning "his powerful word" (TNIV, NIV, NET, HCSB, GNT, NRSV). The NASU's "hope of His calling" in Ephesians 1:18 seems to suggest that believers hope they will be called by God. But believers are already called! The genitive here means "the hope to which you were called" (TNIV, NIV, NRSV, ESV).

Consistent use of the preposition "of" to translate the genitive case represents a misguided attempt at literalism. Clarity in translation demands that the translator consider carefully the meaning of the text in each particular context (see further examples in chap. 5).

In these examples readers might be able to work out the meaning of the genitive by reflecting on the sentence. "The word of his power" is perhaps comprehensible, but it is far from *clear*. At the beginning of this chapter we used the Spanish example *¿Cómo se llama?* No translator would render this in a strict literal manner, "How yourself call?" But in an attempt to stay literal one might say, "How do you call yourself?" While this translation is (barely) comprehensible, it is certainly not clear. Any normal English speaker would say, "What's your name?" Formal equivalent versions have a tendency to alter the forms of the original until they are just comprehensible. Unfortunately, what is comprehensible to a translator may be obscure, awkward, or even meaningless to the average reader.

Clarity can also refer to making explicit what is implicit in the Hebrew or Greek text. This is particularly important when the original readers would have immediately recognized the implicit meaning, but many modern readers would not. In the example of tassels cited earlier (Matt. 23:5), the Greek literally reads "they enlarge the tassels." The TNIV and other versions—including a number of literal ones—clarify that these are the tassels "of their garments" (cf. NIV, GNT, KJV, NKJV, NASU). Similarly, in Luke 18:13, the tax collector in the temple "beats his chest" as he prays. The NLT clarifies that he beat his chest "in sorrow."

The opening phrase of Luke 1:26, "In the sixth month ..." is open to misunderstanding. Is this the sixth month of the year or the sixth month of Elizabeth's pregnancy? The context makes it clear that it is the latter, but a reader could easily miss this. A number of versions, therefore, clarify by translating "In the sixth month of Elizabeth's pregnancy" (TNIV, NET, NLT, GNT, GW). By clarifying the meaning of the text these versions have made the translation more precise and so more accurate.

Natural

Clarity concerns whether a text is readily understandable. A translation may be clear, however, but not natural. A missionary who was translating the Bible for a tribal language in Guatemala often asked his tribal consultants whether a particular phrase he had translated was clear to them. They would usually say "Yes." But if he then asked, "Is that how you would say it?" they would laugh and say "No!" They would then give him an idiomatic alternative. The translation may have made sense, but it was not natural. Consider various English translations of Acts 11:22, where the church in Jerusalem hears about missionary success in Antioch:

> "The report of this came to the ears of the church in Jerusalem."
> (ESV; cf. NKJV, NASU)
> "News of this reached the ears of the church at Jerusalem." (NIV, TNIV; cf. HCSB)
> "A report about them came to the attention of the church in Jerusalem." (NET)
> "When the church at Jerusalem heard what had happened." (NLT)
> "The church in Jerusalem heard about all of this." (NCV)

None of these versions is actually word-for-word. The Greek, translated literally, is something like "but the word was heard into the ears of the church, the one being in Jerusalem ..." All of the versions significantly modify the Greek forms. Yet both the formal (ESV, NKJV, NASU) and mediating versions (NIV, TNIV, HCSB; except NET) retain the Greek idiom "the ears of the church" (*ta ōta tēs ekklēsias*). While this phrase is comprehensible, it is not normal English. No one would ever say "this came to my ears," but rather "I heard about this," or "the news reached me." What sounded natural to the original hearers sounds odd and awkward in the translation.

Examples like this create tension for the translator. By using normal idiomatic English, translators risk missing something in the original meaning. But if they stay literal, they risk obscurity and inaccuracy. In either case nuances can be lost (remember: something is always lost in the translation). This is especially sobering when we consider this is God's inspired Word—his message to humanity.

Translators bear a great responsibility to get it right. J. B. Phillips, who produced an idiomatic English version some sixty years ago, recognized the gravity of this task. He wrote that while translating the New Testament he "felt rather like an electrician rewiring an ancient house without being able to turn the mains off."[4] In this climate, translators must practice balance, discernment, and a good dose of humility when making these difficult decisions.

Audience-Appropriate

A final criterion for excellence in translation serves as a qualifier for the other three. A translation should be appropriate for its intended audience. We must remember that the ultimate goal of translation is not to transfer words from one page to another, but to communicate a message from one person to another. A translation is truly successful only when its readers (or hearers) actually get that message.

This immediately confirms the need for different kinds of translations. It also confirms that the first task of translators is to determine who their target audience is. This could be children, young people, adults, church-goers, unchurched people, new believers, or those for whom English is a second language. Ideally, one version would be perfect for everyone. But this is usually not possible. Versions that use simple vocabulary and short sentences are especially appropriate for children, for those with limited reading skills, and those who speak English as a second language (see NIrV, ICB). Functional equivalent versions are ideal for young people, new Bible readers, and for anyone reading larger units of text to follow the sweep of the biblical story (NCV, CEV, GNT, NLT, GW). Mediating versions are excellent multipurpose Bibles for reading and study (TNIV, NIV, NET, HCSB, NAB, NJB), and formal equivalent versions are par-ticularly helpful for seeing the structure and cadence of the Hebrew and Greek (NRSV, NASU, ESV, RSV, NKJV). No Bible version can do every-thing, and the wealth of resources available today should be viewed as an asset rather than a liability.

Finally, it should be noted that some people reject the use of easy-to-read versions because they claim that some of the meaning of the original text is inevitably lost. This point, as we have seen, is debatable, and it could be argued that idiomatic versions are actually more accurate. But allowing for the moment that some versions oversimplify the text and thereby miss some of the meaning, does this really negate their value?

Consider the following scenario. One reader picks up a formal equiva-lent version and reads Paul's letter to the Romans, understanding about 50 percent of what he reads. Another person picks up a children's version like the NIrV and reads the same letter, comprehending about 95 percent of what she reads. One might well ask, who walks away with a greater knowledge of God's Word? The point is that whatever inadequacies an idiomatic version may have are far outweighed by the benefits of hearing and comprehending God's Word.

For Further Reading

Beekman, J., and J. Callow. *Translating the Word of God.* Grand Rapids: Zondervan, 1974.

De Waard, J., and Eugene A. Nida. *From One Language to Another: Func-tional Equivalence in Bible Translating.* Nashville: Nelson, 1986.

Nida, Eugene A., and C. R. Tabor. *The Theory and Practice of Translation.* Leiden: Brill, 1969.

Scorgie, Glen G., Mark L. Strauss, and Steven M. Voth, gen. eds. *The Challenge of Bible Translation: Communicating God's Word to the World.* Grand Rapids: Zondervan, 2003.

Part 2

Making Words Work

Chapter 3

Translating Words

Words are rather slippery things. A word can mean one thing in one context and something entirely different in another. Consider the word "clip." In the sentence, "clip the coupon to the newspaper," it means to *fasten* something; but in the sentence, "clip the coupon from the newspaper," it means to *remove* it. A candle can "put out" (= generate) light; but you can also "put out" a candle (= extinguish it). To "dust" can mean to remove something ("dust the furniture") or to add something ("dust the crops"). "With" can mean alongside ("England fought with France against Germany") or against ("England fought with France").[1]

One particular linguaphile (a "lover of language") summarizes just how "crazy" English can be:

> Let's face it: English is a crazy language. There is no egg in eggplant or ham in hamburger, neither apple nor pine in pineapple. English muffins were not invented in England or french fries in France. Sweetmeats are candies, while sweetbreads, which aren't sweet, are meat.
>
> We take English for granted. But if we explore its paradoxes, we find that quicksand can work slowly, boxing rings are square, and a guinea pig is neither from Guinea nor is it a pig. And why is it that writers write, but fingers don't fing, grocers don't groce, and hammers don't ham? If the plural of tooth is teeth, why isn't the plural of booth beeth? One goose, two geese. So, one moose, two meese?
>
> If teachers taught, why didn't preachers praught? If a vegetarian eats vegetables, what does a humanitarian eat? In what language do people recite at a play and play at a recital? Ship by truck and send cargo by ship? Have noses that run and feet that smell? Park on driveways and drive on parkways? How can a slim chance and a fat chance be the same, while a wise man and a wise guy are opposites?
>
> When a house burns up, it burns down. You fill in a form by filling it out and an alarm clock goes off by going on. When the stars

are out, they are visible, but when the lights are out, they are invisible. And why is it that when I wind up my watch, I start it, but when I wind up this essay, I end it?[2]

Words don't always mean what you might expect. And the meaning of words is determined by their context. In a famous passage from chapter 6 of Lewis Carroll's *Through the Looking Glass*, Alice accuses Humpty Dumpty of using the word "glory" in an inappropriate way, and Humpty Dumpty responds:

> "There's glory for you!"
>
> "I don't know what you mean by 'glory,'" Alice said.
>
> Humpty Dumpty smiled contemptuously. "Of course you don't—till I tell you. I meant 'there's a nice knock-down argument for you!'"
>
> "But 'glory' doesn't mean 'a nice knock-down argument,'" Alice objected.
>
> "When I use a word," Humpty Dumpty said, in rather a scornful tone, "it means just what I choose it to mean—neither more nor less."
>
> "The question is," said Alice, "whether you can make words mean so many different things."
>
> "The question is," said Humpty Dumpty, "which is to be master—that's all."

Alice is, of course, right. You cannot make words mean whatever you want. Communication would completely break down. Yet there is some truth in what Humpty Dumpty says. Speakers and writers give words their meaning by how they use them. And word meanings can change over time. Evidence of this is the fact that the eleventh edition of Webster's dictionary published in 2003 added 10,000 new words and definitions—and that is since 1998! This slippery and changing nature of words creates a special challenge for Bible translators.

Lexical Semantics: Words and Their Meanings

The basic building blocks of any language are its words. To understand translation we must understand how words work. Linguists use the term *lexeme* to refer to a word understood as a unit of vocabulary. A lexeme is the form of the word you would look up in a dictionary. For example, "make" is one lexeme, but it takes various forms in different contexts (make, makes, made, making, etc.). The study of word meanings is known as *lexical semantics*. Here are some principles of lexical semantics that are essential for accurate Bible translation.

(1) *Words (lexemes) can have many different meanings.* Most words in any language don't have one "literal" or all-encompassing meaning. They have what is called a *semantic range*—a range of potential senses. The reason for this is that languages have a limited number of words to express an almost infinite number of ideas. Many words must do double, triple, quadruple (or more) duty. Consider the English word "key." Probably the first meaning most readers think of is "an unlocking tool." But consider some of the other senses of the word:

Definition	Example
an unlocking tool (n.)	*I lost my key.*
the solution to something (n.)	*What is the key to the puzzle?*
an answer sheet for an exam (n.)	*Check your answers with the key.*
a button on a computer keyboard or typewriter (n.)	*Press the delete key.*
musical tone or pitch (n.)	*What key is that song in?*
a low, offshore island (n.)	*He lives in the Florida Keys.*
main or primary (adj.)	*What was his key point?*

So what is the "literal meaning" of "key"? The answer is *all* of these (and many more). Or, more accurately, *none* of these. "Key," like most words, does not have a literal meaning. It has a semantic range—a range of potential senses. The same is true of words in every language.

Since "unlocking tool" is the first meaning many people consider, we might call this the lexeme's *primary sense.* The primary sense is the most common meaning of a word as it is used by a particular group or in a particular body of literature. But a primary sense is *not* a literal meaning. And the primary sense can change depending on the context. For a group of musicians the primary sense of "key" might be "musical pitch." But for a basketball player it would probably be "the area between the base line and the foul line."

Consider this concept now with respect to the Greek lexeme *logos.* Some might mistakenly say *logos* "literally" means "word." But consider the many ways this lexeme is translated (in italics)—even in a "literal" version like the NASU:

"except for the *reason* of unchastity" (Matt. 5:32)
"But let your *statement* be, 'Yes, yes'" (Matt. 5:37)
"Whoever speaks a *word* against the Son of Man" (Matt. 12:32)
"a king who wished to settle *accounts*" (Matt. 18:23)

"I will also ask you one *thing*" (Matt. 21:24)

"this *story* was widely spread" (Matt. 28:15)

"spread the *news* around" (Mark 1:45)

"He was stating the *matter* plainly" (Mark 8:32)

"I will ask you one *question*" (Mark 11:29)

"His *message* was with authority" (Luke 4:32)

"This *report* concerning Him went out" (Luke 7:17)

"Give an *accounting* of your management" (Luke 16:2)

"Therefore this *saying* went out among the brethren" (John 21:23)

"The first *account* I composed, Theophilus" (Acts 1:1)

"he was the chief *speaker*" (lit. "the one who leads with words"; Acts 14:12)

"have a *complaint* against any man" (Acts 19:38)

"had given them much *exhortation*" (Acts 20:2)

So what is the literal meaning of *logos*? Word? Reason? Statement? Account? Thing? Story? News? Matter? Question? Message? Complaint? Exhortation? And all these meanings of *logos* are found in a formal equivalent version! A functional equivalent version would provide even more choices. The point is that *logos* does not have a literal meaning. It has a semantic range of meanings.

Consider an example from the Old Testament. The Hebrew verb *amar* is translated in the ESV with at least eleven different words in the book of Genesis alone: "said," "spoke," "told," "answered," "commanded," "added," "directed," "named," "thought," "asked," and "replied." In many other cases the word is left untranslated and replaced with quotation marks (to indicate that something was said).

The application of this principle of multiple meanings to Bible translation should be obvious: *Translators cannot translate words "literally"; they must translate them according to their meaning in context.*

(2) This brings us to a second fundamental principle of lexical semantics: *Context determines which meaning is intended.* The meaning of "key" in each of the examples above was determined not by its literal meaning but by the context in which it appeared. "He sang off key" confirms that the reference is to musical pitch. "He shot the ball from inside the key" would alert the hearer to a basketball context.

A speaker or writer chooses the lexeme that best communicates a particular sense in that context. Consider another biblical example. The Greek lexeme *charis* has a semantic range that includes "grace," "favor," "credit," "goodwill," "gift," "thanks," "kindness," and so on. Note how *charis* is translated (in italics) in the following sentences in the NIV:

"For it is by *grace* you have been saved, through faith." (Eph. 2:8)

"Do not be afraid, Mary, you have found *favor* with God." (Luke 1:30)

"If you love those who love you, what *credit* is that to you?" (Luke
    6:32)
"Would he *thank* the servant because he did what he was told to do?"
    (Luke 17:9)
"He gave Joseph wisdom and enabled him to gain the *goodwill* of
    Pharaoh." (Acts 7:10)
"They urgently pleaded with us for the *privilege* of sharing." (2 Cor.
    8:4)

First-year Greek students are often told that *charis* means "grace,"
and grace is usually defined as "undeserved favor" (see Eph. 2:8). But
this is only part of the story. *Charis* can also mean *"deserved* favor." Notice
in the example above that Joseph earned the favor (*charis*) of Pharaoh.
Charis does not have a literal meaning; it has a semantic range—and the
context determines which sense the author intended.

Of course the same is true for the English word "grace." Although
the theological *concept* of grace may mean "undeserved favor," the *word*
can mean many things. You can "say grace" (= a prayer of thanksgiving)
before meals. A person can dance with "grace" (= elegance) or act towards
others "with grace" (= in a dignified manner).

The fact that most words do not have a literal meaning is important
for translators to recognize. It would be inappropriate to insist on using
one English word for each word in the source language. Consider our
example "key." Translating into Spanish requires a *different* word for each
sense:

English	Spanish
an unlocking tool	*llave*
a solution to a puzzle	*clave*
musical pitch	*tono*
a computer button	*tecla*
an island	*cayo*

There is no one-to-one correspondence between English and Spanish,
or between English and Hebrew or Greek. Bible translators must therefore be in a constant mode of interpretation, sensitive to which meaning
senses of a word are being used. Remember our principle from chapter
two: *All translation is interpretation.* The translator must first determine
the meaning of the Hebrew or Greek term in its context. Then he or she
must find an English word, phrase, or clause that reproduces that meaning as accurately and clearly as possible. It is not enough to say that *logos*

means "word." In many contexts it does not. A more technical way to say this is that the semantic range of the Greek lexeme *logos* only partially overlaps with the semantic range of the English lexeme "word." Translating "literally" (i.e., one-to-one) is unreliable.

(3) A third important principle is that *all lexical choices are approximations of meaning*. When I say "in this context *charis* means 'grace,'" I am rendering a judgment about the closest English equivalent in a particular context. *Charis* may carry nuances in this sentence that "grace" does not, and vice versa. Furthermore, there may be two or more English words that function as well in this context—say, "grace" and "favor." Or one word may capture one nuance of *charis* slightly better, while the other captures another nuance. The selection of words often entails a measure of imprecision and ambiguity.

This principle is, again, important for translators. There is not always a "right" translation for a particular Hebrew or Greek word or phrase. While some renderings are certainly better than others, and translators must constantly seek the best option, two or more synonyms might work equally well in a particular case. As always, the goal of translation is not to duplicate the *form* of the original but to reproduce its *meaning*.

(4) This relates to a fourth principle of lexical semantics: *Words may be synonymous, or nearly synonymous, in some contexts but not in others*. There is seldom if ever exact synonymy between words, either within a language or across languages. Consider the words "house" and "home." I could say "he builds homes" or "he builds houses" and mean the same thing. The words are synonymous in this context. But if I said, "She turned that house into a home," I would mean two different things. "House" still means the building itself, but "home" now means "a place of love and security."

In some contexts, the Greek lexemes *sarx* and *sōma* mean essentially the same thing, the physical body. In Ephesians 5:29 (NIV), Paul says that "no one ever hated his own body [*sarx*], but he feeds and cares for it." This is essentially the same as the primary sense of *sōma*, as in Matthew 10:28: "Do not be afraid of those who kill the body [*sōma*]." In many other contexts, *sarx* carries the negative sense "sin nature" or "fallen humanity," which *sōma* does not have. Their semantic ranges overlap in some contexts but not in others. The same thing happens across languages. The sense of the English lexeme "grace" may overlap in some contexts but not in others with the Greek lexeme *charis*. The principle again is that translation is not a mechanical replacement of words. It is a careful and measured assessment of their meaning in context.

(5) A fifth important principle of lexical semantics is that *the meaning of words changes over time*. In the English language, this is most easily demonstrated with the King James Version. First published in 1611, the KJV is the most enduring English translation of all time. Yet the KJV

is outdated both in terms of its Greek text (see chap. 8) and its archaic language.

One of the authors was sitting in a chapel service several years ago when the speaker read from James 5 in the KJV. The reader came to verse 11 and read, "The Lord is very pitiful." The author looked up startled, but nobody in the service seemed to notice this apparently heretical statement! (perhaps a sad indictment on the lack of attention given to the public reading of the Word). Of course in 1611, when the KJV was published, "pitiful" meant "full of pity" or "compassionate." The TNIV translates the phrase, "the Lord is full of compassion."

There are many examples of archaic language in the KJV. James 2:3 speaks of a man entering the church assembly wearing "gay" clothing. While to the original translators this meant fancy or expensive, the primary sense of "homosexual" today makes this rendering inappropriate. Most translations use "fine clothes" (TNIV) or something similar. Some KJV words are simply obscure: *wotteth, staves, discomfited, hind, holpen, knop, mar,* etc. Others are misleading, such as "pitiful" or "gay." To communicate most accurately and clearly, translators should use contemporary rather than archaic English, and translations should be revised periodically to reflect language changes. In light of this reality, we will discuss language changes related to gender in chapter 7.

Of course there is a flip side to this principle. Translators should also avoid language that is too contemporary or slangy. The "hip" language used in translations like *Black Bible Chronicles* or *The Word on the Street* quickly becomes outdated. Within a few years it sounds silly rather than contemporary. Translators should also avoid language that is peculiar to a particular sociolinguistic group. The NEB was rightly criticized for being too *donnish,* that is, reflecting the language idiosyncrasies of British university professors.

Collocations

The differences in word meanings between languages is especially evident when we consider *collocational relationships.* These are meanings achieved through a word's relationship with another word (its *collocate*). For example, what can you "make" in English? You can make pancakes, make trouble, make sergeant, make sense, make a shirt, make friends, make a plane (= catch), make a deal, make a difference, make a vow, make love, make a law, make someone leave, and make Paris in one day (= reach Paris in a day). This illustrates the principle that words can have many different meanings. But it also shows that a word's meaning is determined by its collocational relationship with other words.

This is significant for translation since these relationships change—often radically—between languages. For example, in Spanish the most common word for "take" is *tomar*. Yet you do not "take a walk" in Spanish, you "give a walk" (*dar un paseo*). Spanish uses a different collocation to express the same meaning. In English you "take care," but in Spanish you "have care" (*tener cuidado*). In English you "take a trip," but in Spanish you "make a trip" (*hacer un viaje*). In English, a drug "takes effect," but in Spanish it "supplies effect" (*surtir efecto*).

The point is that it is impossible to translate "make," "take," "have," "give," "keep," or hundreds of other collocates literally into Spanish, since Spanish collocations are considerably different from English ones. You first must interpret the meaning of the collocation in the source language and then find a phrase or idiom that matches it in the receptor language. *All translation is interpretation.*

One of the authors once asked a missionary linguist working in Irian Jaya if his tribal language had many idioms. His response was, "The idioms aren't too bad, but the collocations are a nightmare!" The point was that deceptively simple statements about going, taking, keeping, making, and so on did not match up to their English counterparts and so could not be translated literally.

The same is true for the biblical languages. For example, we teach beginning Greek students that the Greek verb for "make" or "do" is *poieō*. Yet *poieō* does not provide an adequate translation for most of the collocates mentioned above. In Greek you do not make trouble, make a difference, make a vow, make love, or make a deal. The converse is also true. There are many collocates with *poieō* that make (!) little sense in English. Below is a sampling of contexts in which *poieō* appears with various collocates. We have translated it "literally" in the middle column and then given an English translation on the right. These are taken from the ESV to show that even a translation that claims to be "essentially literal" or "word-for-word" cannot translate collocations literally. This is a small sampling of just one lexeme.

Reference	"Literal" rendering of *poieō*	ESV rendering
Matt. 3:8	*Make* fruit	*Bear* fruit
Matt. 5:32	*Make* adultery	*Commit* adultery
Matt. 6:1	*Make* righteousness	*Practice* righteousness
Matt. 6:2	*Make* alms	*Give* to the needy
Matt. 13:23	*Make* fruit	*Yield* fruit
Matt. 13:41	*Make* lawlessness	*Be* a lawbreaker

Matt. 20:12	*Make* one hour	*Work* one hour
Matt. 21:43	*Make* fruit	*Produce* fruit
Matt. 22:2	*Make* a feast	*Give* a feast
Matt. 26:18	*Make* the Passover	*Keep* the Passover
Matt. 26:73	Your accent *makes* you evident	Your accent *betrays* you
Matt. 28:14	*Make* you secure	*Keep* you out of trouble
Mark 3:14	*Make* Twelve	*Appoint* Twelve
Mark 4:32	*Make* great branches	*Put out* large branches
Mark 6:21	*Make* a dinner	*Give* a banquet
Mark 15:1	*Make* a council	*Hold* a consultation
Mark 15:15	*Make* sufficient the crowd	*Satisfy* the crowd
Luke 1:51	*Make* power	*Show* strength
Luke 1:68	*Make* redemption	Redeem (*poieō* untranslated)
Luke 1:72	*Make* mercy	*Show* mercy
Luke 2:48	*Make* us thusly	*Treat* us so
Luke 12:33	*Make* for yourself purses	*Provide* yourselves with purses
Luke 12:47	*Make* to his will	*Act* according to his will
Luke 13:22	*Make* a journey	Journey (*poieō* untranslated)
Luke 15:19	*Make* me as a hired one	*Treat* me as ... a servant
Luke 16:8	Because he *made* shrewdly	For his shrewdness (*poieō* untranslated)
Luke 18:7	*Make* the vengeance	*Give* justice
John 3:21	*Make* truth	*Do* the truth
John 5:11	*Make* healthy	Heal (*poieō* untranslated)
John 5:27	*Make* judgment	*Execute* judgment
John 7:4	*Make* in secret	*Work* in secret
John 7:19	*Make* the law	*Keep* the law
John 11:37	*Make* not that he might die	*Keep* him from dying

John 16:2	*Make* you from synagogues	*Put* you *out* of the synagogues
John 17:4	*Make* the work	*Accomplish* the work
Acts 1:1	*Make* word	*Deal* with
Acts 5:34	*Make* the men outside	*Put* the men outside
Acts 7:19	*Make* their infants exposed	Expose their infants (*poieō* untranslated)
Acts 7:24	*Make* vengeance	Avenge (*poieō* untranslated)
Acts 10:33	*Make well* to come	*Kind enough* to come
Acts 15:3	*Make* great joy to all	*Bring* great joy to all
Acts 15:33	*Make* time	*Spend* some time
Acts 20:24	*Make* my life precious	*Account* my life of any value
Acts 24:12	*Make* pressure a crowd	*Stir up* a crowd
Acts 24:17	*Make* alms	*Bring* alms
Acts 25:3	*Make* an ambush	*Plan* an ambush
Acts 27:18	*Make* a casting out	*Jettison* the cargo

So what does *poieō* "literally" mean? Make? Do? Bring forth? Practice? Give? Perform? Commit? Keep? Appoint? Hold? Form? Satisfy? Accomplish? Show? Treat? Take? Execute? Indulge? Even translators of formal equivalent versions must acknowledge that *poieō* can mean any of these things (and many more), depending on its context and collocations.

This brings us back to the fundamental point made in chapter 2: meaning must always take precedence over form. The literal translator recognizes that *poieō* often does not mean "make," but still argues that, as much as possible, the same English word should be used for each word in Hebrew and Greek. But there is no justification for this. If the goal of translation is *meaning*, then the correct question is not, "Is 'make' an adequate translation?" but rather "What English word, phrase, or idiom *best* captures the sense of the collocation?"

Formal equivalent versions tend to seek one-to-one correspondence, and if the translation works—even awkwardly—then that translation is retained. The problem is that this results in unnatural English. For example, the Hebrew verb *nathan* usually means "give." Yet the word appears in many collocations that are impossible to translate literally into English. Other collocations translate only awkwardly. Consider the following examples, where *nathan* is translated as "give" in a formal equivalent version (here the NKJV).

Reference	"Literal" collocation (from NKJV)	Idiomatic English
Gen. 43:14	Give you mercy	Grant/show you mercy
Ex. 21:23	Give life for life	Take a life for a life
Deut. 23:14	Give your enemies over to you	Deliver your enemies over to you
1 Kings 1:48	Give one to sit on the throne	Appoint one to sit on the throne
2 Chron. 32:11	Give you to die by famine	Allow you to die by famine
Ps. 72:1	Give the king your judgments	Endow the king with your justice
Isa. 3:4	Give children to be their princes	Make children their princes
Isa. 50:6	Give My back to those who struck Me	Offer my back to those who struck me
Isa. 55:4	Give him as a witness	Make him a witness
Jer. 25:31	Give the wicked to the sword	Put to death the wicked by the sword
Mic. 7:20	Give truth to Jacob	Be true to Jacob

Although the NKJV's translations above are *comprehensible*, they are neither *clear* nor *natural*. This is because the collocation was translated literally instead of according to its most natural English equivalent.

Wordplays and Verbal Allusions

While it is important to translate words according to their meaning in context, there are times when the *form* of a word carries certain aspects of meaning. This is especially so with wordplays and verbal allusions. Many wordplays are difficult, if not impossible, to reproduce in English since they are based on the spelling or sound of Hebrew and Greek words.

For example, in Isaiah 5:7 the prophet says that the Lord "looked for justice, but saw bloodshed; for righteousness, but heard cries of distress" (TNIV). In the original text this is a play on words, since the words for "justice" and "bloodshed" (*mishpat*; *mispach*) have similar sounds in Hebrew, as do the words for "righteousness" and "distress" (*tzedaqah*; *tze^caqah*). Translators are hard-pressed to reproduce this kind of wordplay, since it is based on the coincidental similarity of Hebrew words. They would have to find English words that both sound alike and have the correct meaning. Another missing wordplay in the English text is in Genesis 2:7, where "the LORD God formed a man from the dust of the ground." The Hebrew words for "man" (*^ʾadam*) and "ground" (*^ʾadamah*) are similar. It would be difficult, if not impossible, to find English parallels.

One of the few cases where a Hebrew wordplay works well in English is in Genesis 2:23. The Hebrew text says that Eve would be called *^ʾishah* ("woman") because she was taken out of *^ʾish* ("man"). Just as the word *^ʾishah* is a derivative of *^ʾish*, so the word "woman" is a derivative of "man." Of course, while this (coincidentally) works in English, it would not work in many other languages. Even the Septuagint (the Greek Old Testament) misses the wordplay, since the Greek words for man (*anēr*) and woman (*gynē*) used in Genesis 2:23 do not sound alike.

Verbal echoes and allusions are also difficult to reproduce in translation. Some words that are verbally similar in Greek or Hebrew may not be in English. For example, Greek uses the same root for the noun "faith" (*pistis*) and the verb "believe" (*pisteuō*), something English readers cannot see. Similarly, the Greek words commonly translated "righteousness" (*dikaiosynē*) and "justification" (*dikaiōsis*) are related to the same root form in Greek (they are "cognates"), but their English translations are not.

Another kind of verbal allusion occurs when a later use of a word recalls an earlier one, linking the passages in some way. In 1 Corinthians 3:10 Paul identifies himself as a "wise [*sophos*] master builder" (NASU, NKJV), who has laid the foundation for the Corinthian church. Many versions recognize that "wise" is not a normal English adjective to describe a builder and so translate *sophos* more idiomatically as "skilled" (ESV, HCSB, NRSV) or "expert" (NLT, NIV, CEV, GNT). While these accurately represent the meaning of *sophos* in context, they lose an important verbal allusion. In 1 Corinthians 1–4, Paul has repeatedly used the adjective *sophos* ("wise") and the noun *sophia* ("wisdom") to contrast the true wisdom of God with the false wisdom of the world. A "wise" builder is therefore one who builds on God's wisdom, which is found in a crucified Messiah. While the NIV used "expert," the TNIV recognized the verbal allusion by using "wise." Retaining the allusion was deemed theologically important and so worth the slightly less idiomatic English.

A similar situation appears in the parable of the rich fool (Luke 12:13–21), where formal equivalent versions pick up a wordplay with the Greek term *psychē*. In verses 19–20 the rich man speaks, and God responds:

> "And I will say to my soul [*psychē*], 'Soul [*psychē*], you have many goods laid up for many years to come; take your ease, eat, drink, and be merry.' " But God said to him, "You fool! This very night your soul [*psychē*] is required of you." (NASU; cf. NKJV, ESV)

Psychē can mean many different things, and functional equivalent versions render it with various expressions: "life," "soul," "person," "self," "mind," etc. The TNIV translates "I'll say to myself" in verse 19, and "your life will be demanded from you" in verse 20. Both of these are accurate translations in context, but they miss the verbal play with *psychē*. In this case idiomatic English was viewed as more important than a minor play on words. As always, translators must make difficult decisions concerning which aspects of meaning are most important to retain in translation.

Trying to reproduce an author's vocabulary and style can create this same kind of tension for the translator. Mark is fond of the Greek adverb *euthys* (forty-two times) and uses it to give his Gospel a fast-paced, action-oriented style. *Euthys* can mean many different things, and meaning-based versions like the TNIV translate it with various expressions: "just as" (1:10), "at once" (1:12, 43), "without delay" (1:20), "when" (1:21), "just then" (1:23), "quickly" (1:28), "as soon as" (1:29), "immediately" (1:42; 2:8). Sometimes the word simply indicates a transition to the next scene and so is left untranslated (1:30). The NASU, by contrast, consistently renders *euthys* as "immediately" (forty times). While this often misses the meaning of the word in context, it mimics Mark's style and so enables the reader to pick up some of the flavor of his fast-paced narrative. Something is lost, but something else is gained.

These examples reveal some of the dilemmas translators face. Because languages are different, it is not always possible to translate words according to their closest English equivalent *and* retain verbal allusions and wordplays. Translators must constantly make difficult choices and seek appropriate balance, judging which structural features should be retained and which may be sacrificed. Unfortunately, something may be lost in the translation. This is another good reason to use more than one version and to choose translations from across the translation spectrum. Formal equivalent versions sometimes sacrifice readability and equivalent meaning-in-context to retain verbal allusions. Functional equivalent versions capture the meaning better, but may lose nuances associated with the formal structure of the language.

Technical Theological Terms

Another difficult issue related to translating words is what to do with technical theological terms. Advocates of formal equivalence argue that traditional renderings like "justification," "sanctification," and "propitiation" should be retained since they are rich in theological meaning. Advocates of functional equivalence often assert that these terms are incomprehensible to average readers and so clearer English should be utilized. The NIV and TNIV retain "justifies/ justification" for *dikaioō/ dikaiosis* (Rom. 4:25; 5:16, 18), while the NLT, GNT, and NCV speak of being "made right with God" (CEV: "made acceptable to God"). The NIV, TNIV, NET, NLT, GW, and others utilize "holiness" or "made holy" for the traditional "sanctification" (*hagiasmos*; Rom. 6:19, 22; cf. 1 Cor. 1:30; 1 Thess. 4:3, 4, 7; 2 Thess. 2:13; Heb. 12:14). Other functional equivalent versions speak of "living for God" (NCV) or "belonging completely to him" (CEV).

Cautions are in order for both formal and functional versions. Functional equivalent versions must be careful not to distort the meaning of the original by leaving out important nuances of meaning. Formal equivalent versions must recognize that if readers do not understand the meaning of the text, then the translation has failed.

Consider the many difficulties surrounding the translation of the Greek term *hilastērion* in Romans 3:25:

"whom God put forward as *an expiation*" (RSV)
"whom God put forward as *a propitiation*" (ESV)
"whom God displayed publicly as *a propitiation*" (NASB, NASU)
"God presented him [Christ] as *a sacrifice of atonement*" (NIV, TNIV)
"God sent him *to die in our place to take away our sins*" (NCV)
"For God presented Jesus *as the sacrifice for sin*" (NLT, rev. ed., 2004)
"For God sent Jesus *to take the punishment for our sins and to satisfy God's anger against us*" (NLT, 1st ed., 1996)

The Greek cognates *hilastērion* (Rom. 3:25; cf. Heb. 9:5), *hilasmos* (1 John 2:2; 4:10), and *hilaskomai* (Heb. 2:17) come from the language of the Old Testament sacrificial system. Often in the Greek Old Testament (the Septuagint) and in Hebrews 9:5, *hilastērion* refers to the "mercy seat" or the "atonement cover" of the ark of the covenant. This was the place where sacrificial blood was sprinkled on the Day of Atonement (Lev. 16:14). The NET Bible thinks this is the meaning here and translates Romans 3:25, "God publicly displayed him at his death as the mercy seat." Most scholars, however, think that word is being used figuratively, meaning the place of atonement or the sacrifice itself.

There has been a historical debate over whether these *hilas-* terms should be translated "expiation" or "propitiation." The former carries the general sense of satisfaction for sins through an atoning sacrifice, while the latter includes both meaning senses, a sacrifice of atonement and the appeasement of God's wrath. The 1952 RSV was criticized for changing the KJV's "propitiation" to "expiation," presumably leaving out the dimension of the appeasement of God's wrath. Other formal equivalent versions have sought to "correct" this by returning to the KJV's "propitiation" (NASB, NASU, ESV, NKJV).

But is this an appropriate solution? Very few readers—even Christian readers—have any idea what "expiation" *or* "propitiation" means! Of course they could consult a dictionary; but a standard computer dictionary does not include the noun "propitiation" and defines the verb only as "to appease or conciliate somebody or something" (Microsoft Encarta Dictionary). A standard desk dictionary—the 1,500 page Webster's II—gives only the definition "to appease." This means even the most literate readers would miss the sense of "a sacrifice to pay for sins," unless they consulted either a larger dictionary or a Bible commentary. One has to question whether "propitiation" is an adequate *English* translation if readers cannot even determine its meaning by looking it up in a dictionary!

The NIV and TNIV (cf. NRSV) try to be more intelligible by using "sacrifice of atonement." This is better, but many readers will still not understand what "atonement" is. The NCV ("to die in our place to take away our sins") and the revised (2004) NLT ("as the sacrifice for sin") are certainly clearer. The first edition of the NLT (1996) is the most explanatory, describing both punishment for sins and appeasement of wrath.

The long and short of all this is that there is no perfect solution, and translators will continue to grapple with bridging the gap between the biblical world and our own. The best solution, however, is probably not to use obscure Latin-based terms (like "propitiation"), which are meaningless to most readers and which, in any case, have no etymological connection to the Greek terms being used (in this case, the *hilas-* roots).

Another difficult question concerning technical language—touched on briefly earlier (p. 50)—is how to render the Greek term *sarx*. Formal equivalent versions have traditionally translated the word "flesh." While this works for those who have grown up hearing and reading Bible language, it does not represent standard English. The English word "flesh" is commonly used of (1) soft body tissue, (2) the meat of animals, (3) the pulpy part of a fruit or vegetable, and (4) in special idioms like "flesh and blood." The Greek word *sarx* has a much wider range of senses, including "body tissue," "physical body," "living being," "human being," "human nature," "natural descent," "earthly life," "human realm of existence," "sexual impulse," "sinful human nature," as well as other nuances.

The situation is complicated by the specialized use of the term in Paul. *Sarx* serves for Paul as a technical term for the eschatological concept of the old age of existence characterized by sin and death that is now superseded by the new age of salvation inaugurated by Christ. To be "in the flesh" is to live in the old realm; to be "in Christ" is to live in the new.

There is no single English word that captures well this complex concept, whether "flesh" (KJV, NKJV, RSV, NRSV, ESV), "sinful nature" (NIV, TNIV), "old nature" (NLT), "sinful selves" (NCV), "corrupt nature" (GW), or "human nature" (GNT). All solutions have their unique problems. Those versions that refer to a "nature" (sinful/old/corrupt/human) may miss the eschatological connotations of the term and wrongly introduce the idea of two natures. Those that use the traditional "flesh" may be susceptible to an inappropriate Platonic or Gnostic dichotomy between mind/spirit and matter. Because the English lexeme "flesh" has—through centuries of use—become for Christian readers a technical term with most of the same connotations as Greek *sarx*, translations produced for Christian readers may choose to retain this term. Other versions with a broader audience will want to find alternatives.

As you come to the end of this chapter, you may wonder whether *any* translation can get it absolutely right. The answer is both no and yes, depending on whether one keeps the word "absolutely." If we were to change that to "essentially right," then the answer is a positive yes. Our concern throughout has been to illustrate the inherent difficulties of translation from one language to another, but we want to conclude by encouraging you regarding the accuracy and reliability of your English Bible. The examples shown in this chapter confirm again the basic principles set out in chapter 2: that meaning must take precedence over form, and that insisting on a "literal" translation of words is neither desirable nor possible. At the same time, versions from across the translation spectrum can provide different nuances of form and function and so are useful tools for students of God's Word.

For Further Reading

Cotterell, P., and M. Turner. *Linguistics and Biblical Interpretation.* Downers Grove, IL: InterVarsity Press, 1989.

Nida, Eugene A., and J. P. Louw. *Lexical Semantics of the Greek New Testament.* Atlanta: Scholars, 1992.

Silva, M. *Biblical Words and Their Meanings: An Introduction to Lexical Semantics.* Rev. ed. Grand Rapids: Zondervan, 1995.

Chapter 4

Translating Figurative Language: Idioms, Metaphors, and Poetry

Some years ago, when Eastern Europe was still under Soviet control, one of the authors of this book and his wife spent most of one summer speaking and teaching in churches and seminaries in the "Iron Curtain" countries. Although many of the students and pastors knew English as a second language, many others did not; so the issue of communication became a matter of special concern—especially because the professor's language was laced with a profusion of idioms, many of which were not at all understandable to second-language people. To his utter chagrin, but to the delight of many later on, the wife of the accompanying missionary couple kept a list of his idioms (two pages long) and then showed them to him! *His* problem was that English was his first language, and probably no language in history uses as many idioms as does modern English.

For *biblical translators* this problem plays in reverse; that is, how does one transfer the idioms of two dead languages (ancient Hebrew and Koine Greek) into modern English, while trying to be faithful to both languages? It is fair to say that idioms represent some of the greatest challenges for a translator.

An *idiom* may be defined as "an expression whose meaning cannot be understood from the combined meanings of its individual words." It goes without saying (an idiom!) that you cannot translate idioms literally if you hope to retain their meaning. Suppose a traveling businessman says to his colleague, "By the way, I'm hitting the road at the crack of dawn." Consider how a "literal" translation of this might sound:

Idiom	"Literal" translation
By the way	Along the path
I'm hitting the road	I'm striking the street
at the crack of dawn	at the fissure of sunrise

Such literal renderings of idioms don't communicate accurately because idioms don't "mean" what they "say." An accurate translation of the sentence above would be something like, "I wanted to let you know that I am leaving very early in the morning." Although the original idioms are lost, not to mention some of the "color" of the language, the meaning is retained. The challenge for a translator is to determine the meaning of the idiom in the original language, and then to identify a different idiom or other wording in the receptor language that means the same thing.

To help get the point across, consider the following "short story," count the number of American English idioms (all beginning with an "s"), and then think of how one might "translate" this into plain English — or German or French(!):

"Idiomania"

My career had seen better days. I was skating on thin ice, scraping the bottom of the barrel, and ready to say uncle. The boss and I did not see eye to eye, and he told me to shape up or ship out. There was no silver bullet. It was a safe bet I was going to sink or swim. Nobody could save my bacon. My smart-aleck colleague was a stick-in-the-mud and a snake in the grass who would sell me down the river as soon as shake a stick at me. I could smell a rat, so I steered clear of him. I had one slim chance. It was a shot in the dark, but if I could keep a stiff upper lip, stick to my guns, and sail close to the wind, I would get a second chance. The saving grace was that at the last minute I got a second wind and was saved by the bell.

A literal translation of this would be completely meaningless, since the story has nothing to do with skating, thin ice, barrels, uncles, eyes, bullets, bets, swimming, bacon, and so on.

Translating Biblical Idioms

The Bible contains hundreds of Hebrew and Greek idioms. Many of these make no sense when translated literally. For example, in John 10:24 the people ask Jesus (literally), "Until when will you take up our souls?" The Greek idiom "take up souls" means to "keep in suspense," so even the NASU translates, "How long will You keep us in suspense?" Similarly, in John 9:21 the parents of the man born blind tell the religious leaders that their son "has lifespan." This idiom means he is "of age" (NASU, TNIV, ESV) or "old enough" (NJB, GNT, CEV) to speak for himself. (Notice that "of age" is an English idiom.) Mark 1:32, translated literally, says that Jesus healed all "those having badly." The Greek idiom means "those who were sick." In cases like these, even formal equivalent versions must abandon a literal policy and translate idiomatically.

Other Hebrew and Greek idioms may be comprehensible when translated literally, but result in awkward or obscure English. First Samuel 10:9 (ESV) reads, "When he [Saul] turned his back to leave Samuel, God gave him another heart." The Hebrew idiom "give a new heart" means "to change one's disposition or heart attitude." Most versions read "God changed his heart" (NASU, HCSB, TNIV). Esther 1:14 (ESV) speaks of the close advisers to King Xerxes "who saw the king's face." The Hebrew idiom means those "who had special access to the king" (cf. NASU, TNIV, NIV, NRSV, HCSB).

In Joshua 10:6 (ESV) the men of Gibeon say to Joshua, "Do not relax your hand from your servants." The Hebrew idiom "relax your hand" means to "abandon," and most versions say "do not abandon your servants" (NASU, HCSB, NRSV, TNIV, GW, NET; cf. NKJV). Mark 1:2 NKJV reads, "I send my messenger before Your face." "Before your face" is a Greek idiom which means "ahead of you," and most versions translate accordingly (HCSB, NET, NIV, TNIV, NAB, GNT, GW). While the original NASB used "before your face," its 1995 update (NASU) revises this to "ahead of you." The NRSV similarly revises the RSV. The ESV retains the awkward "before your face."

In cases like these, the reader may be able to figure out the idiom by thinking about it for awhile. But what was clear and natural to the original readers now sounds strange and awkward. Consider the common Hebrew and Greek idioms "answered and said," which introduce many quotations in both Old and New Testaments. The idiom does not describe two actions—"answered" *and* "said"—but one. It simply means that the person "answered." In attempting to translate word-for-word, formal equivalent versions produce unnatural (and sometimes misleading) English. Compare the following versions at the beginning of Genesis 27:37:

"Isaac *answered and said* to Esau" (ESV, NKJV, NASB)
"Isaac *answered* Esau" (NIV, TNIV; cf. GNT)
"Isaac *replied* to Esau" (NET, NJB, NASU; cf. NAB)

No English speaker today would say "he answered and said to me." All of the functional equivalent versions (GNT, CEV, GW, NCV, NLT) and the mediating ones (NIV, TNIV, HCSB, NET, NAB) recognize the idiom and translate it simply "answered" or "replied." While the original NASB used "answered and said" 186 times in the Old and New Testaments, its revision (NASU) uses it only 75 times, usually replacing it with "replied." The revisers evidently recognized that this was a Hebrew idiom, not an English one. Oddly, while the RSV correctly interpreted the idiom as "answered" in all but seven instances, its revision called the ESV reintroduced "answered and said" sixty-one times in the Old Testament (but never in the New Testament).

Here is a sampling of more idioms from the Old and New Testaments. We have noted a formal equivalent version in the center column and a more idiomatic translation on the right.

Reference	Formal equivalent	Idiomatic translation
Exod. 32:19	Moses' anger burned (NASU)	Moses became extremely angry (NET)
Deut. 5:6	Egypt ... the house of slavery (NRSV)	Egypt ... the place of slavery (HCSB)
Deut. 20:8	hearts melt (NASU)	dishearten (NIV, TNIV)
2 Kings 2:7	the sons of the prophets (ESV)	the prophetic guild (NET)
Esth. 2:21	sought to lay hands on (NKJV)	plotted to assassinate (NLT, NET)
Job 33:16	[God] opens the ears of men (NASU)	[God] gives a revelation to people (NET)
Ps. 11:6	the portion of their cup (ESV)	what they deserve (NET)
Ps. 41:9	lifted the heel against me (NRSV)	turned against me (NLT, NET)
Matt. 1:18	she was ... with child (ESV, NIV)	she was ... pregnant (TNIV, NET)
Mark 4:5	It had no depth of soil (NKJV)	the soil was shallow (NIV, TNIV)
Mark 12:20	the first took a wife (ESV)	the first married (NRSV)
Heb. 1:3	the word of his power (ESV)	his powerful word (NRSV)
1 Peter 1:13	gird your minds for action (NASB)	prepare your minds for action (NASU)

In cases like these, the more literal rendering is usually comprehensible, but it is not clear or natural. No one today under forty, and not raised on Scripture, would ever say that they are going to "take a wife" or that a woman is "with child." Others would do so only as a light-hearted echo of the biblical language on which they were raised.

Deciding whether a Hebrew or Greek idiom is normal English can sometimes be tricky business (an idiom, by the way). This is especially so because of the profound impact the KJV has had on the English language. Some idioms have entered English precisely because they were translated literally in the KJV. Second Chronicles 36:13 says that King Zedekiah "stiffened his neck" against turning to the Lord (NASU, RSV, ESV, NRSV, NKJV). This Hebrew idiom means he became stubborn or rebellious. Since "stiff-necked" appears in an English dictionary (= "extremely obstinate and arrogant"), the NIV, TNIV, and NAB chose to retain the idiom, translating that Zedekiah "became stiff-necked." Other versions translate idiomatically as "obstinate" (HCSB) or "stubborn" (NET, CEV, GW), presumably assuming that for most readers a stiff neck requires a chiropractor rather than a repentant heart.

There are some cases where retaining even an awkward idiom picks up an important wordplay in the original text. For example, in Genesis 40:13 Joseph interprets the dream of Pharaoh's former cup-bearer, telling him that Pharaoh will "lift up your head" and restore him to his former position in the royal court. The Hebrew idiom "lift up your head" here means "release" (GW), "reinstate" (NET), or "pardon" (GNT, CEV). These are all legitimate translations. Yet a few verses later (40:19), Joseph tells the imprisoned baker that Pharaoh will also "lift up your head—from you!—and hang you on a tree" (ESV). The same Hebrew idiom now means to execute. In order to capture this play on words, many versions retain the unusual idiom "lift up your head" in both verses (NAB, NJB, HCSB, NKJV, NASU, NRSV). The NIV and TNIV astutely use "lift off your head" in the second. Here, as elsewhere, translators must make difficult decisions about which features of the text should be retained and which may be sacrificed for greater clarity.

Metaphors and Similes

Communication is made more interesting and colorful by using comparison. There are many figures of speech in Scripture that use comparison: metaphors, similes, analogies, parables, allegories, and so on. Similes are explicit comparisons between two things, using the words "like" or "as": "People are like sheep." In metaphors the two things are directly equated so that the comparison is implicit rather than explicit: "People are sheep."

The metaphors and similes of Scripture can present challenges for Bible translators, especially for those working in tribal contexts. In a tropical region where snow is unknown, the statement that God will make your sins "as white as snow" (Isa. 1:18) would be meaningless. The rule translators generally follow in such contexts is that if the comparison is single-faceted (the comparison here being only the color of snow), then a different metaphor may be used, or if none can be found, the translation can be made without a comparison. This verse could be translated "as white as cotton," use the name of a white flower, or simply be "very white." In contexts where "white" implies racial superiority, the phrase could be translated "very clean." Little is lost since the only point being made concerns cleanness or purity.

However, if the metaphor is multifaceted, it should be retained (perhaps with explanatory notes describing what it is). For instance, sheep play a critical role in Scripture: "The LORD is my shepherd" (Ps. 23:1); sinners are like lost sheep (Isa. 53:6; Luke 15:4); Jesus is the Lamb who was slain (Rev. 5:6). To remove these metaphors in a culture where sheep are unknown would have implications for many passages and so does harm to the overall message of the Bible. The best solution here is to retain the metaphor and educate people about the nature of sheep.

These cultural issues are less of a concern in contemporary English versions, since translators can assume a basic knowledge of many biblical cultural items. Most modern readers are familiar with biblical things like sheep, camels, wolves, lamps, swords, and the like. But less common items are another matter, which we will discuss along with other kinds of difficult cultural questions in chapter 6.

For the sake of simplicity, some English versions occasionally reduce the metaphors of Scripture to abstractions. In 2 Samuel 22:2 the Lord is called "my rock, my fortress." Most English versions retain both metaphors, but the GNT translates "my rock" as "my protector." While this may be helpful for younger children or people at a simpler reading level, most readers can quite easily comprehend the metaphor. Our opinion is that translators should retain such metaphors whenever possible.

Similarly, in Matthew 6:3 the metaphorical idiom "do not let your left hand know what your right hand is doing" is rendered by the CEV as "don't let anyone know about it," and by the NCV as "don't let anyone know what you are doing." These versions are explicitly geared toward readers with limited reading and comprehension skills, for whom the metaphor was evidently deemed too difficult. Almost all other versions retain the metaphor.

One compromise solution for versions geared toward remedial readers is to add a clarifying word or phrase. In the example above from 2 Samuel 22:2, the CEV includes both the metaphor and the abstract meaning: "my mighty rock, my fortress, my protector." Similarly, while the first edition of the NLT (1996) translated "spare the rod" in Proverbs 13:24

with the abstraction, "refuse to discipline your children," the 2004 revision reintroduced the metaphor with an explanatory phrase, "spare the rod of discipline." This kind of translation both retains the metaphor and helps the reader comprehend it.

Live versus Dead Metaphors

Although we recommend retaining the metaphors of Scripture as much as possible, there is an important exception: when the metaphor is dead rather than live. A live metaphor illustrates a point with a concrete image, which continues to be evoked in the mind of readers. In the phrase "God is my rock," the reader considers the characteristics of a rock and then determines which features apply to the subject and which do not. God is not "hard," but he is "strong." God is not a material object, but he is a source of protection. A dead metaphor, by contrast, has lost its concrete image in the minds of readers, who move directly to the abstract meaning. Consider the following metaphorical idioms in English:

He drove the point home.	That's a piece of cake.
She lost face.	My salary is chicken feed.
That's the last straw.	She cried her eyes out.
That's just sour grapes.	He changed his mind.
She gave him the cold shoulder.	We must not lose our heads.
We got our butts kicked!	That is a far cry from what I actually said.
That's as easy as pie.	He is fed up.
Don't hold your breath.	You need to make a clean break.

In these and many others, the reader's mind goes directly to the abstract meaning without pausing to think about the metaphorical "picture." The first idiom means something like "he made his argument well." Readers would not first envision either driving or a home. "She lost face" means "she lost social status." No reader would envision a face disappearing. Nor would readers normally picture straw, grapes, bottoms, shoulders, pies, cakes, chickens, minds, beheadings, or distant shouting with these other idioms. The metaphors have become so familiar that the reader does not consider the concrete image but moves directly to the abstract meaning. These are dead metaphors. Translated literally, they do not communicate well to readers of a different language. "That's as simple as a dessert pastry" would be a poor translation of "that's as easy as pie"!

Here are some dead metaphorical idioms of Scripture, which even formal equivalent versions recognize as dead.

Reference	Literal idiom	Meaning (see RSV, NASU, etc.)
Matt. 10:27	"hear in the ear"	"hear whispered"
Matt. 22:16	"look at people's faces"	"swayed by appearances"
Mark 2:19	"sons of the bridechamber"	"wedding guests"
Mark 9:42	"millstone of a donkey"	"great millstone"
James 1:23	"face of his birth"	"natural face"
James 3:6	"wheel of birth"	"course of life"

The challenge for translators is to determine whether a metaphor is live, dead, or somewhere in between. In Luke 1:69 Jesus is identified as a "horn of salvation in the house of ... David" (NASU, TNIV, HCSB, ESV). Some versions translate this as a "mighty Savior from the royal line of David" (NLT) or something similar (cf. GNT, CEV, GW, NCV). The image of a horn comes from the Old Testament and originally signified the horns of powerful animals like a ram or ox. But by the first century this may have been a dead metaphor, so that hearers would have thought immediately of something "mighty" or "powerful" (cf. Ps. 18:2). Similarly, the phrase "house of David" would not conjure up a home, but rather a dynastic line of kings. In this case, the translation "a mighty Savior from the royal line of ... David" (NLT) may be exactly what a first-century reader would have envisioned.

Consider also Ephesians 5:2 (NASU), where Paul tells believers to "walk in love" (cf. ESV, HCSB, NKJV). The Greek idiom "walk in ..." means to live life by certain standards, and so the NIV renders the idiom "live a life of love" (cf. TNIV). The NET Bible and NAB say "live in love." Some have criticized these translations, since (it is claimed) the Hebrew mind viewed life as a journey and Paul here pictures believers "walking" down the path of life. While this is possible, in this context it is unlikely. Like the English idiom "walk the talk," the Greek idiom ("walk in ...") was probably dead in contexts like this and was heard by its original readers simply as "live this way."

Sometimes formal equivalent versions will translate metaphorical idioms as literally as possible in order to capture "all of the meaning." But what is forgotten is that idioms don't mean what they say. This would be like translating the English idiom "by the way" as "along the path" and then explaining that the speaker is viewing life as a journey, picturing himself along life's path. While this is a nice thought, it is simply wrong. To the English speaker "by the way" is simply an idiomatic way of saying, "I want to say something else."

Since translators are not reading Hebrew or Greek as native speakers, there is a tendency to force a literal sense on metaphors and idioms that were never intended to be heard that way. Once again this creates a challenge for translators. Careful study of the historical and literary contexts is necessary. A good rule of thumb (another idiom!) is that if similar images commonly appear beside the metaphor (e.g., images related to paths, walking, or journeying; cf. Psalm 1), then it is probably live. If not, it is probably dead.

Once again, all translation involves interpretation, and decisions must be made on a case-by-case basis concerning whether the metaphor is live, dead, or somewhere in between. The translator cannot simply "play it safe" by retaining all metaphors, since turning a dead metaphor into a live one introduces meaning into the text that the original author did not intend.

The Extended Metaphor: Poetry

One of the more remarkable features of being human is our ability (often propensity) to communicate not only with the straightforward language of everyday speech, but also with poetry, the "language of the heart." Because poetry is a deliberate attempt to communicate at a level of emotive language beyond mere prose, this can be the most difficult to transfer into a receptor language. Here especially, it is often true that "something is lost in translation."

This reality can pose special difficulties for Bible translators, since well over one-third of the Hebrew Bible comes to us in the form of poetry (Job, Psalms, Proverbs, much of the prophets). There are good reasons for this. The majority of people for whom the Old Testament was written did not themselves read, but were read to; and for several reasons poetry is much more easily memorized than prose. So while translating Hebrew poetry into English may not be as difficult, for example, as translating Shakespeare into German, it nonetheless poses special problems for the translator.

These problems were articulated in the first "How to" book as threefold. First, as already noted, poetry by its very nature is intentionally emotive in a way that prose is not. Second, the psalms in particular are *musical* poems that functioned in Israel the way hymn books have traditionally functioned in the church. Third (and now the point of this chapter), the vocabulary of poetry is purposely metaphorical.[1]

For the translator, these realities pose problems of both structure and meaning. We will illustrate these from one of the best-known psalms, Psalm 23.

Structure

Almost all scholars recognize that the poems that make up the Hebrew Psalter have various forms of structure, just as is true of the various poems of English poets. Classical English poetry was dictated by both rhyme and meter. For example, the prologue of Alfred Lord Tennyson's "In Memoriam" contains eleven quatrains (stanzas of four lines each), which have a structural pattern of *a b b a* and a rhythmic pattern of four beats to a line, starting with an offbeat. It thus begins (with markers added):

a	Strong Son´ of God,´ Immor´tal Love,´
b	Whom we,´ that have´ not seen´ Thy face,´
b	By faith,´ and faith´ alone´ embrace, ´
a	Believ´ing where´ we can´not prove;´

While none of us would ever be so pedantic as to cite it with this stress pattern so obvious, it is nonetheless the deliberate pattern that holds the entire poem together: all eleven quatrains have this same pattern.

Hebrew poetry, on the other hand, is almost never expressed with "rhyme." Rather, while tending to have lines of similar length and stress, it is most noticeable for its patterns of parallelism, either "synonymous" (where two lines say the same thing in different ways), "antithetical" (where the second line is the opposite of the first), or so-called "synthetic" (where the second, and sometimes third, build upon the first).

This parallelism can make the discovery of units within a psalm more difficult. Although a growing consensus has emerged as to what constitutes a unit within a given psalm, differences of analysis will always exist. For example, at issue in Psalm 23 is the placement of verse 4, which the KJV rendered: "Yea, though I walk through the valley of the shadow of death, I will fear no evil: for thou art with me; thy rod and thy staff they comfort me." Some translations (RSV, NRSV, ESV) set this verse off as a separate unit, thus dividing the psalm into three stanzas. Others place verse 4 at the beginning of verses 5 and 6 (NASU, NAB). This is problematic because all of verses 1–4 are held together by the pastoral imagery of a shepherd with his sheep, while in verses 5–6 the poet reflects on enjoying hospitality and protection as a guest in the house of Yahweh. Thus, most contemporary versions, on the basis of this content, divide the psalm into two parts, verses 1–4 and 5–6 (TNIV, GNT).

Meaning

In some ways Psalm 23 may not be the best place to illustrate translating meaning since it is one of the best-known psalms in the English Bible. Translators are reluctant to alter the well-known phrases of the KJV. At the same time, this very reluctance may be used to demonstrate the challenges of translating Hebrew poetry. We select three lines from the poem to illustrate how retaining traditional language can sometimes be at odds with accurately reproducing meaning.

First, in verse 1, the "I shall not want" (KJV), which is retained in versions in the KJV line of revision (ASV, RSV, NASB, NRSV, ESV), has been changed to something more meaningful in almost all other English versions. The problem is that "want" is rarely used anymore to express the concept of being in need. If a person "wants" in today's English, that person "desires" something, whereas the Hebrew means "I lack nothing" (TNIV, NJB; cf. REB, NAB). The GNT puts it positively: "I have everything I need" (cf. NLT). Our point here is that the Hebrew meaning is quite clear, and when translated into idiomatic English, one keeps both the poetry and the meaning.

Second, in the fourth line, which spells out "how" Yahweh is the poet's good shepherd, the KJV speaks of being led "in the paths of righteousness." This rendering exposes the difficulty of the Hebrew construct relationship between two nouns, to be discussed briefly in chapter 5. Is it to be understood as qualitative, that is, "paths characterized by righteousness," or descriptive, indicating the shepherd's care in leading his sheep in the "right paths"? As before, the KJV tradition has tended to stay with the traditional interpretation (ASV, RSV, NASB, ESV), as did the NIV. The NRSV in this case broke ranks and joined most other modern English translations in rendering it "right paths" (TNIV, HCSB, NET, REB, NAB, NLT, GNT). The reason for this is easy to see: the traditional rendering "paths of righteousness" adds a religious dimension to a pastoral poem (green pastures, quiet waters, refreshes me). The more recent tendency is to stay with the pastoral imagery of sheep being led by a shepherd along the "right paths."

Third, "walk through the valley of the shadow of death" is perhaps the most difficult phrase in the psalm to translate. Even the KJV translators included a marginal note, "Read *deep gloom*, and so elsewhere." The difficulty lies with the Hebrew word *tzalmawet*, which ordinarily means "deep shadow" or "deep darkness" (as in Jer. 2:6, NRSV, ESV; cf. TNIV "utter darkness"), but which was rendered "in the midst of the shadow of death" in the Septuagint. Versions within the KJV tradition usually retain "shadow of death," with a footnote to "the darkest valley" (ASV, RSV, NASB, ESV). Other contemporary versions reverse this, translating "the darkest valley" in the text (NRSV, REB, NAB, TNIV, GNT), often with a note to "shadow of death."

In conclusion, the aesthetic and symbolic nature of poetry presents unique challenges for the translator. Poetry that uses rhyme or assonance is especially difficult, since words with equivalent meanings across languages seldom also share formal features (like rhyme or assonance). This is less of a problem with Hebrew poetry, which is characterized primarily by parallelism of content rather than by rhyme. The greatest challenge when translating Hebrew poetry is to determine the meaning of figurative language and then find appropriate cultural parallels in the receptor language.

Other Figures of Speech

Rhetorical Questions

Just as metaphors don't always "mean what they say," so other figures of speech also function in nonliteral ways. Questions, for example, can be *real questions* requesting information ("How old are you?") or *rhetorical questions* that serve many other purposes. The question "Are you crazy?" when someone performs a dangerous stunt does not expect an answer, but is a way of saying "You are acting crazy!" "Don't you think I know that?" is an expression of frustration or indignation. "Will you stay for dinner?" is not a question but an invitation, meaning "Please stay for dinner." "Isn't that beautiful?" functions as an exclamation, "That's beautiful!"

The Bible has many rhetorical questions that function in a variety of ways. In John 11:9 Jesus says, "Are there not twelve hours of daylight?" This packs more rhetorical punch than the bland statement, "There are twelve hours of daylight." Many rhetorical questions provide emphasis. When Paul says, "Shall we sin because we are not under law but under grace?" (Rom. 6:15), he means, "We should certainly not sin ..." "How can Satan cast out Satan?" (Mark 3:23) means "Satan surely cannot cast out Satan."

Rhetorical questions can emphasize facts that are obviously true or untrue. Pilate says in John 18:35, "Am I a Jew?" meaning "I am certainly not a Jew!" Paul says, "Is Christ divided?" (1 Cor. 1:13) meaning Christ is not divided. Rhetorical questions can also express commands or rebukes. "Why are you bothering this woman?" (Matt. 26:10) means "Stop bothering this woman." "Why are you so afraid?" (Mark 4:40) means "Don't be afraid" or "You should not be so afraid." Rhetorical questions can also replace conditional clauses. "Is any one of you sick?" (James 5:14) means "If any one among you is sick ..."

Rhetorical questions can present challenges for Bible translators, since some languages do not use rhetorical questions or use them very differently than in the Bible. Jesus' statements "Why are you so afraid?" or "How can Satan cast out Satan?" would be seriously misunderstood if interpreted as requests for information. This is less of a problem with English versions, since, as with metaphors, English uses rhetorical questions in many of the same ways as Hebrew and Greek.

English versions geared especially toward children or remedial readers occasionally translate rhetorical questions as statements. For example, the rhetorical question "Who can forgive sins but God alone?" (Mark 2:7) is rendered by the NCV as "Only God can forgive sins," and "Why trouble the teacher any more?" (Mark 5:35) as "There is no need to bother the teacher anymore." The goal here is to avoid misunderstanding for young readers or for those for whom English is a second language. (The NCV arose from a version originally designed for the deaf community.) As we have emphasized throughout this book, different Bible versions serve different purposes; so it is appropriate to have versions with adjusted rhetorical questions for readers for whom they are difficult to understand.

Hyperbole, Irony, and Sarcasm

Like idioms and rhetorical questions, other figures of speech will be misunderstood if taken literally. *Hyperbole* is exaggeration intended for dramatic effect. It is hyperbole when the women of Jerusalem sing that "Saul has slain his thousands, and David his tens of thousands" (1 Sam. 18:7 TNIV). Both numbers are hyperbolic and form a Hebrew poetic parallelism indicating great prowess in battle. Matthew relates that the Messiah's birth disturbed King Herod "and all Jerusalem with him" (Matt. 2:3). Obviously, not every person in Jerusalem heard the news. Jesus uses hyperbole when he says that the scribes and Pharisees "strain out a gnat but swallow a camel" (Matt. 23:24).

Irony occurs when the apparent meaning of a statement is contrary to its real meaning. *Sarcasm* is usually ironic, but is also intended to mock or deride. Jesus' statement to the religious leaders in Mark 7:9 is both ironic and sarcastic: "You have a fine way of setting aside the commands of God in order to observe your own traditions!" (TNIV). The CEV captures this sarcasm well: "You are good at rejecting God's commands so that you can follow your own teachings!"

Paul similarly mocks his opponents in Corinth when he says, "Already you have all you want! Already you have become rich! You have begun to reign—and that without us!" (1 Cor. 4:8 TNIV). Although the Corinthians had great pride in their spirituality, they were in fact spiritually immature. At Jesus' trial, the soldiers sarcastically mock Jesus: "And they began to call out to him, 'Hail, king of the Jews'" (Mark 15:18 TNIV). This statement is both sarcastic and ironic. Jesus' enemies sarcastically mock him, but the Christian reader knows he is indeed king of the Jews.

In most cases the average English reader will understand that these are figures of speech by reading them in context. Functional equivalent versions occasionally add a clarifying word or phrase to make the meaning clear. For example, the NLT adds the word "taunted" in Mark 15:18: "Then they saluted him and taunted, 'Hail! King of the Jews!'" The CEV similarly reads that "They made fun of Jesus and shouted, 'Hey, you king of the Jews!'" This is a case of making explicit what is implicit in the text. We will see more examples of this in chapter 6 on language and culture.

Synecdoche and Metonymy

As with metaphors, figures of speech like synecdoche and metonymy make language more colorful and interesting. *Synecdoche* occurs when a part is used for the whole, or vice versa. "He owns a nice set of wheels" uses a part (wheels) to describe the whole (a car). "California just passed a new law" uses the whole (California) to refer to a part (the state legislature). *Metonymy* occurs when one thing is used for something related to it. "The pen is mightier than the sword" means that ideas are ultimately more effective than military force. "The White House released a statement" refers to a press release from the executive branch of the United States government.

There are many examples of both synecdoche and metonymy in the Bible. When Jesus says "the Son of Man has no place to lay his head" (Matt. 8:20 TNIV), he means he has no home of his own. This is synecdoche: a place to lay his head represents a home. That Job "did not sin with his lips" (Job 2:10 NASU) means that he "did not sin in what he said" (TNIV). This is metonymy: lips are associated with speaking. To "die by the sword" (Jer. 11:22 TNIV) means to "die in battle" (NLT, CEV). The "hand of the LORD" can refer to the power of the Lord (1 Kings 18:46; Acts 11:21) or judgment from the Lord (Ex. 9:3).

Formal equivalent versions almost always retain literal translations of synecdoche and metonymy. Functional equivalent versions sometimes clarify them. In 1 Kings 18:46 the NLT translates "the hand of the LORD was on Elijah" as "the LORD gave special strength to Elijah." Mediating versions tend to translate synecdoche and metonymy literally unless they are considered too obscure or nonstandard English. The TNIV, HCSB, and NET all translate "sin with his lips" in Job 2:10 as "sin in what he said." TNIV and HCSB retain "die by the sword" in Jeremiah 11:22, while the NET renders the metonymy "killed in battle" (with a footnote giving a literal translation).

Conclusion

When translating idioms, metaphors, and other figures of speech, the goal should be the same as with all good translation: *to preserve as much of the meaning as possible for the target audience.* For idioms (which don't mean what they say) this involves finding a different, but equivalent, idiom in the target language. When there is no equivalent idiom, it means simply translating the idiomatic meaning without using figurative language.

For metaphors, translators must first determine whether that metaphor is live or dead. Live metaphors retain the concrete "picture" in the mind of the original readers and so can be preserved in translation. Dead ones have lost that image and so should be replaced with an equivalent metaphor or idiom in the target language.

Figurative language like that surveyed in this chapter is often closely linked to particular social and cultural situations. For example, using the American English idiom "couch potato" assumes a cultural context where people sit (or lie!) on couches while watching television. Culture and language can be closely related. In chapter 6 we will pursue additional translation challenges that arise when moving from the biblical cultures to our own.

For Further Reading

Caird, G. B. *The Language and Imagery of the Bible.* Philadelphia: Westminster, 1980.

Ryken, Leland. *Words of Delight: A Literary Introduction to the Bible.* Grand Rapids: Baker, 1992.

Chapter 5

The Greek Genitive: A Problem of Its Own

Although nouns and verbs are basic to all languages, they are formulated differently from language to language. For example, in English we "conjugate verbs" in the present tense by adding an "s" in the third person singular and, primarily, by adding "-ed" in the past tense. Otherwise we use "modals" such as "will," "have," and "had" to express other tenses. For nouns English changes form only in the possessive singular (with 's) and in the plural. Greek, on the other hand, changes forms much more often, for both nouns and verbs. In contrast to English, Greek is a highly inflected language, meaning that both nouns and verbs have different forms that serve different functions.

One of the greatest challenges in this regard is translating the Greek genitive case, which is the case used not only to express possession (as the English pronouns, "my, her, his, your, our, their"), but also to express a great many other relationships. This makes translation of the genitive into English difficult, because in many cases we have no exact equivalent. That same thing can be said of what is called the construct relationship between two Hebrew nouns.

Historically, the habit has been to use the English preposition "of" for the construct construction in Hebrew or the genitive case in Greek (as in "the word *of God*"); and many who think of themselves as translating "literally" consider this to be its "literal meaning." But in fact it is simply one English way of trying to approximate the meaning of the Greek genitive. The problem can be illustrated in the following figure, where the meaning of the Greek genitive overlaps only in part with the English prepositional phrase, "of + NOUN."

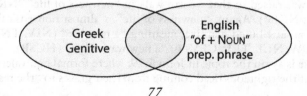

Unfortunately, the traditional use of "of + NOUN" as the default translation for the Greek genitive often creates something ambiguous in English that was not ambiguous in Greek. In other cases, the resulting translation is not only ambiguous, but obscure and misleading.

The purpose of this chapter is to illustrate the challenges of translating the Greek genitive case and in this way to demonstrate, once again, the point that *all good translation involves interpretation*. Translators must carefully consider the meaning of each genitive *in context* and must translate using the best English equivalent. In many cases, "of + NOUN" works perfectly well as a translation of the genitive. For example, phrases like "the genealogy of Jesus Christ," "the son of David," "the Word of God," and "the land of Israel" all make good sense in English and accurately reproduce the meaning of the genitive.

In other cases the translation of the genitive with "of" is a good choice since it approximates the ambiguity of the Greek text. For example, in Revelation 1:1 the translation "the revelation of Jesus Christ" could mean a revelation given *by* Jesus Christ (a subjective genitive), or a revelation *about* Jesus Christ (an objective genitive). The NLT chooses the former: "the revelation *from* Jesus Christ." Yet both subjective and objective genitives fit well the purpose and content of the book, and many scholars suggest that the author is being intentionally ambiguous. Thus, it seems best to render the phrase "the revelation of Jesus Christ" (NIV, NET, HCSB, GW, ESV, etc.).

Similarly, in Romans 1:17 the genitive phrase "righteousness of God" could mean God's own righteousness (a character trait), or it could mean righteousness *from* God, which God bestows on believers. While the original NIV chose the latter ("the righteousness from God"), its revision the TNIV returned to the ambiguous "the righteousness of God," leaving the reader with either or both options (cf. NET, NAB, NASU, NKJV, ESV).

In many other cases, however, translation of a genitive with "of" is misleading. We have already seen several examples of this in chapter 2 (pp. 38–39). Here are a few more. In Ephesians 1:17, Paul prays that God, "the Father of glory" (ESV, NRSV, NASB, NKJV), will give wisdom to the Ephesians. But what does "Father of glory" mean? This is probably an attributive genitive, meaning "glorious Father" (NIV, TNIV, HCSB, GW, NLT, TEV, CEV). Similarly, in Romans 6:4 Paul says that Christ was raised so that we can walk in "newness of life" (NRSV, ESV, NASU, NKJV). Again, "newness of life" is almost nonsensical English. This is an attributed genitive, meaning "a new life" (NIV, TNIV, NET, NJB, GW, NLT, TEV, CEV) or "a new way of life" (HCSB).

Life is again the topic in John 5:29, where formal equivalent versions speak of the righteous dead coming from their graves to "the resurrection of life" (NKJV, NASU, ESV, NRSV). This is a genitive of result or destination, meaning "rise to live" (NIV, TNIV), "rise to eternal life" (NLT), or "resurrection resulting in life" (NET). In Romans 1:7, Paul says that the believers in Rome are "loved by God" (NIV, TNIV, HCSB, NET, ESV)—a subjective genitive. In a misguided attempt to be "literal," the NASU and NKJV translate with the awkward "beloved of God." The same thing happens in John 6:45, where the NASU reads that God's people will be "taught of God." Almost all other versions, including most formal equivalent ones, recognize this as a subjective genitive and translate it "taught *by* God." In these and many other cases, defaulting to "of + NOUN" without carefully interpreting the meaning of the genitive in context results in obscure or inaccurate translation.

In the rest of this chapter, we offer a variety of examples of the challenges translators face in rendering the Greek genitive. Our primary purpose is to show that translators must first of all be good *interpreters* of the biblical text. Simply replacing the genitive construction with an "of + NOUN" phrase risks mistranslating God's Word.

Whose "Co-worker"?

Our first illustration is one of the (rare) places where the Greek genitive is *possessive* but does not work well when translated as a possessive in English. This is especially true in some cases where Paul refers to his companions as "co-workers." We have no difficulty when Paul refers to one of them as "*my* co-worker," since in English this means what Paul intended, that he and his companion share ministry in common. But that changes when the possessive is "God," and it is thus rendered "God's co-worker." In English this means that a human being is a *co-worker with God* regarding the gospel. However, in the two instances where Paul says this (1 Cor. 3:9; 1 Thess. 3:2), he intended a true possessive—that two or more *human beings* are co-workers and both *belong* to God.

The first of these occurs in 1 Corinthians 3:9, where Paul writes, "We are God's co-workers; you are God's field, God's building" (TNIV). All three of these phrases are true possessives: Paul and his co-workers belong to God, and so do the Corinthians. But in English the phrase "we are God's co-workers" can only mean that God is working together with these co-workers (Paul and Apollos). This mistaken notion appears in most formal equivalent versions (ESV, NASU, NKJV: "we are God's fellow workers") and some of the mediating ones (TNIV, HCSB: "we are God's co-workers"). The NET gets the meaning right: "We are coworkers belonging to God." The NLT similarly reads, "For we are both God's workers," and the CEV, "Apollos and I work together for God." Here, then, is a place where translating literally leads the English reader to a mistaken idea about what Paul said.

A similar problem appears in 1 Thessalonians 3:2, where Paul identifies Timothy as "our brother and God's fellow worker" (NIV). Again, the meaning of the phrase is that Timothy is *Paul's* co-worker *who belongs to* God. Some versions carry on the mistaken idea that Timothy is a co-worker *with* God (ESV, NASU, NIV, NJB, REB). Others capture Paul's intended meaning with translations ranging from "co-worker *for* God" (NRSV, NAB), to "who works with us for God" (GNT; cf. CEV), to "co-worker in God's service" (TNIV). In these and many other cases, an idiomatic translation is necessary to capture the meaning of the genitive.

Patience of Hope?

Another place where translators have shown reluctance to abandon a nearly meaningless rendition of the genitive occurs in 1 Thessalonians 1:3, where Paul commends these believers for their "faith, love, and hope." In doing so, he puts these three words in the genitive as *modifiers* of "work, labor, and patience." The problem with translating the Greek genitive with an "of" phrase emerges in this case with the word "hope." That is, both "work of faith" and "labor of love" are basically understandable, and the latter has become a common idiom in English. In both cases the mind quickly "translates" these phrases into subjective genitives, where "faith" and "love" find expression in the Thessalonians' labor on behalf of the gospel and for others.

But no native English-speaking person would ever say "patience of hope" (KJV, NKJV), which is only partly eased when "patience" is changed to either "endurance" (HCSB) or "steadfastness" (NASU, ESV, NRSV). No one would say to a friend, "I really appreciate your endurance of hope." For this reason the idiomatic versions turn all three phrases into more recognizable English—"your work produced by faith, your labor prompted by love, your endurance inspired by hope" (NIV, TNIV).

The Word of ...

In English one may speak of "my word" or "the word of life" and be understood in the first instance to be referring to something I said, and in the second to refer to a message that brings, or offers, life. But the same clarity is not true of "the word of the Lord," which may refer either to Scripture (as in "Hear the word of the Lord"), to a message Christ has spoken, or to the message *about* Christ. And since a biblical author probably did not intend all three of these at any given point, translators must make a contextual decision regarding the meaning of the phrase and render it accordingly: either "the Lord's word" (= a message the Lord has spoken), or "the message about the Lord." A third option is to leave the phrase ambiguous ("the word of the Lord") and let the reader decide which meaning is intended.

When Paul tells the Colossians to "let *the word of Christ* dwell richly among you" (3:16), this cannot refer to Scripture, since the New Testament did not exist yet. So at issue for translators is whether this is a subjective genitive (the message from Christ) or an objective genitive (the message about Christ). Here is a case where translators must decide whether to choose one interpretation over another or to leave the passage intentionally ambiguous. The GNT ("Christ's message"), GW ("Christ's word") and the first edition (1996) of the NLT ("the words of Christ") interpret the phrase as a subjective genitive—the message *from* Christ. The NLT (2004), CEV ("the message about Christ"), and HCSB ("the message about the Messiah") favor an objective genitive—the message *about* Christ. Other versions retain the ambiguous "word of Christ" (NIV, NET, NAB, NJB, NASU, ESV) or "the message of Christ" (TNIV), which could be understood as either objective or subjective.

It is of interest that when the same idiom occurs with "God" as the genitive modifier ("word of God"), there is not the same ambiguity. "God" in this case is easily understood as the subject of the action. This is something God has said. Indeed, when Paul says in Romans 9:6 that "God's word" has not failed, he immediately turns to the Old Testament as the "word" to which he is referring. This is probably true also of its occurrences in 1 Corinthians 14:36; 2 Corinthians 2:17; and Colossians 1:25, which are almost universally translated "the word of God" or "God's word."

But when Paul uses this phrase twice in 1 Thessalonians 2:13 ("the word of God, which you heard from us ..."), he is referring to the message about Christ that he had preached among them. So while it is still a "subjective genitive," it now refers to the gospel rather than the Old Testament. To avoid any confusion here, translators would do well to render it "God's message" (cf. NJB, REB, GNT, NLT, NET).

The Fellowship of . . .

Paul's use of the word *koinōnia* with the genitive presents a special difficulty, since *koinōnia* has a wide range of meanings: fellowship, participation, association, sharing. It becomes all the more difficult when the genitive is rendered with an "of," as in 1 Corinthians 1:9 ("*of* his Son"); 10:16 ("*of* the body and blood of the Lord"); 2 Corinthians 13:14 and Philippians 2:1 ("*of* the Spirit"); Philippians 3:10 ("*of* Christ's sufferings"); and Philemon 6 ("*of* Philemon's faith"). Only the extreme, nearly unintelligible, literalism of Young's *Literal Translation* renders each of these as we have in parentheses above, and always as "fellowship of." The KJV tended to do the same, except that the translators switched to "communion of" in 1 Corinthians 10:16 and 2 Corinthians 13:14 (but not in Phil. 2:1), and to "communication of" in Philemon 6 (an archaism that cannot be found in most dictionaries).

Recognizing the obscurity of such "literalism," most contemporary formal equivalent versions offer a variety of idioms, depending on their understanding of the word *koinōnia*. This is especially so for 1 Corinthians 1:9, where it is not clear who is in *koinōnia* with whom. The formal equivalent tradition tends to avoid making a choice by rendering it ambiguously, "the fellowship of his Son" (KJV, RSV, ESV). The NASB broke ranks here by joining the NIV, TNIV, and NAB in rendering it "into fellowship *with* his Son." Most likely the phrase here means something like "communal participation in the sonship of Christ," which the REB seems to come closest to with its "to share in the life of his Son."

Equally difficult for translators is Paul's usage in Philippians 3:10. The traditional but ambiguous "fellowship of his suffering" (KJV, NASB) was changed to "share his sufferings" in the RSV, which was kept in the ESV but changed in the NRSV to "the sharing of his sufferings." The NIV's "fellowship of sharing in his sufferings" was not one of its better moments, so it was changed in the TNIV to what seems most likely to be Paul's intent, "participation in his sufferings."

The passage in Philemon 6 has been especially difficult for most interpreters, including translators, whose renderings range from the literal, but almost meaningless, "the fellowship of your faith" (NASB), to "the sharing of your faith" (RSV, ESV), to "your partnership with us in the faith" (TNIV; cf. NAB), and "the faith you hold in common with us" (REB). These last two seem to be closest to the meaning of the phrase.

Some Conclusions

This chapter has surveyed some of the challenges of translating the Greek genitive case. There is an unfortunate tendency among formal equivalent versions to default to the "of + NOUN" construction without considering carefully the meaning of the genitive in context. Only when this construction clearly misrepresents the sense of the Greek do these versions introduce a different idiom. In other words, they start with *form* and then move to *function*.

There are two problems with this approach. First, this is an artificial "equivalence," since the Greek genitive is a *case form,* while "of + NOUN" is an English prepositional phrase. In other words, the two are *not* formally equivalent. Second, defaulting to an *of*-phrase often produces a translation that, at best, is ambiguous, and, at worst, is obscure and inaccurate. While some translators consider obscurity to be a virtue in Bible translation since it forces readers to make interpretive decisions on their own, obscurity can also lead to misunderstanding and misinterpretation. If the sense of the Greek genitive is clear from the context, why should translators withhold this meaning from readers?

Since the goal of all good translation is to reproduce the *meaning* of the text, translators should carefully consider the function of genitives in context and then find an English translation that adequately captures that sense. In many cases, this will be an "of + NOUN" construction; in others it will not. Sometimes "of" works well because it retains the same measure of ambiguity in English that the genitive has in the Greek (e.g., "the revelation of Jesus Christ"). Yet even here, this is not because the translation is "literal," but because it happens to capture well *the meaning* of the genitive in context. As always, meaning trumps form in Bible translation and translators must first of all be good interpreters of the Word.

For Further Reading

Beekman, J., and J. Callow, *Translating the Word of God* (Grand Rapids: Zondervan, 1974), 249–77.

Wallace, Daniel B. *Greek Grammar beyond the Basics: An Exegetical Syntax of the Greek New Testament.* Grand Rapids: Zondervan, 1996 (esp. 72–136).

Part 3

Translation and Culture

Chapter 6

Cultural Issues in Translation

A missionary in Spain relates an incident where, after a delicious meal at a restaurant, a visiting American friend tried to request "a doggie bag." Using the little Spanish he knew, he asked for *"una bolsa de perro"* (lit., "a bag of dog"). The perplexed waiter wanted to please his customers but had no idea what the man was asking for. Did he mean a bag full of dog pieces? A tote bag for dogs? A bag made of dog skin? The first problem was that the English idiom "doggie bag" cannot be translated literally into Spanish. But the greater problem was that in Spain people simply do not take food home from restaurants. There is no right way to ask for a doggie bag because it isn't socially acceptable to do so.

This story illustrates the fact that language and culture are closely bound together. Translation always involves more than just resolving linguistic differences. It also means crossing the cultural boundaries that divide two worlds. The language of the Bible is steeped in the cultures of the ancient Near East and the Greco-Roman world. To reproduce God's Word effectively, translators must keep one eye on the world of the text and one on the modern world. In chapter 4 we touched on some of the linguistic and cultural issues related to the idioms and metaphors of Scripture. Here we will survey other cultural challenges translators face.

Historical and Cultural Background

Readers approach the Bible from a variety of backgrounds. Some have a great deal of knowledge about the culture and history of the Bible. Others approach the text as relative novices. Translators of contemporary English Bible versions generally assume a basic knowledge of places and things in the biblical world. For example, place names like Israel, Jerusalem, Samaria, Assyria, Babylon, and so on are given without explanation, although Bibles often come with maps. Similarly, the identity of ethnic peoples (Hittites, Philistines, Edomites, Samaritans, etc.) and religious groups (priests, Levites, Pharisees, Sadducees, etc.) are not usually defined. Readers are expected to acquire this kind of general background knowledge by reading through the Bible or from outside sources such as sermons, notes in a study Bible, commentaries, Bible dictionaries, or Bible encyclopedias.

Traditional Bible Language

Some language traditionally used in Bible versions, though familiar to most churchgoers, may be unknown to an unchurched person or to a new Bible reader. We use the word "traditional" here because these terms are not necessarily more literal or formal equivalent, but have become familiar through the long tradition of English Bible translation, especially the KJV.

Functional equivalent translators sometimes seek more common, "everyday" language. The NCV, for example, consistently uses "followers" for the traditional "disciples" (*mathētai*), and the CEV uses "Jewish meeting place" for "synagogue" (*synagōgē*). The term "covenant" is rendered "promise" or "agreement" in some functional equivalent versions (CEV, GW, NCV); others retain "covenant" (NLT, GNT). Israel's "tabernacle"—the portable temple in the wilderness—is identified in some versions as "the Tent" (GNT; cf. CEV, GW) or "the Holy Tent" (NCV); "tabernacle" is retained in the NLT, TNIV, NET, HCSB, and all the formal equivalent versions.

The traditional designation "scribes" (*grammateis* [KJV, RSV, NASU, NRSV, ESV, REB, NAB, NJB]) does not make clear the nature of this first-century Jewish profession, so many versions render the Greek term as "teachers of the law" (TNIV, GNT), "experts in the law" (NET), "teachers of religious law" (NLT), or "teachers of the Law of Moses" (CEV). The "chief priests" (*archiereis*), the upper echelon of the Jerusalem priesthood, is translated as "leading priests" in the NLT and NCV. The "Sanhedrin" (*synedrion*), the Jewish high court, is rendered by functional equivalent versions as the "council" (GNT, CEV, GW), "high council" (NLT), or "Jewish council" (NCV). The mediating versions use "Sanhedrin" (NIV, TNIV, NET, NAB, NJB, HCSB). Curiously, the formal equivalent versions use "council" (NKJV, RSV, NRSV, ESV, NASU), presumably imitating the KJV, which itself used "council." Here is an unusual case where the mediating versions are more "literal" than the formal equivalent ones.

Implicit and Explicit Background Information

Contemporary Bible versions sometimes make explicit what was implicit to the original readers. This may be as simple as adding a clarifying word.

Matthew 3:13 (TNIV) reads, "Then Jesus came from Galilee to the Jordan to be baptized by John." The NET Bible, together with most functional equivalent versions, clarify that this is the Jordan "River" (NET, NLT, CEV, GW). Although the word "river" does not appear in the Greek, adding it helps to clarify the meaning.

In other cases, cultural customs are clarified for readers who may not understand them. In Genesis 37:29 Reuben "tore his clothes" when he discovered that his brothers had sold Joseph as a slave (TNIV, NET, ESV). In Hebrew culture this was a sign of mourning or grief, so functional equivalent versions add that he tore his clothes "in grief" (NLT, GW) or "in sorrow" (CEV, GNT; cf. Mark 14:63). In Exodus 34:13 God commands Israel to "cut down the Asherah poles" of the Canaanites. Some functional equivalent versions clarify the nature of these poles. CEV has "tear down the sacred poles they use in the worship of the goddess Asherah" (cf. GW, GNT). NCV says simply "cut down their Asherah idols."

In the parable of the Pharisee and the tax collector, Jesus says that two men entered the temple to pray, "one a Pharisee and the other a tax collector" (Luke 18:10 TNIV). The NLT describes the latter as a "despised" tax collector. The purpose is to show how Jesus' Jewish contemporaries—who hated tax collectors as Roman collaborators—would have heard his words. A few sentences later, we learn that the tax collector "beat his breast and said, 'God, have mercy on me, a sinner'" (Luke 18:13 TNIV). Again the NLT clarifies that he beat his chest "in sorrow." What was implicit for the original readers is made explicit for modern readers.

Some might object to these expansions, since the words "despised" or "in sorrow" do not appear in the Greek text. While this is true, the meaning that they convey was part of the author's intention and would have been immediately recognized by the original readers. Again we are faced with the dilemma of whether to reproduce the form or the meaning of the original text. If the goal of translation is to transfer as much of the meaning as possible, then implied meaning must be taken into account for readers who would not normally recognize it.

Of course, care must be exercised here, since it is possible to introduce the wrong meaning. The first edition of the NLT (1996) identified the tax collector as "dishonest" rather than "despised." This was inaccurate, since nothing in the parable suggests the man was cheating people. Calling him "dishonest" might also imply that his repentance was insincere, which is the opposite of Jesus' point.

The challenge for translators is to determine how much implicit background material to provide. If too little is given, readers may miss important nuances of meaning; if too much, the translation becomes a commentary. (Since all translation involves interpretation, there is always a fine line between commentary and translation.) In general, translators should include implicit information when there is a significant likelihood that their target audience will miss the cultural or historical significance of an action or statement. The goal should always be to allow the contemporary reader to hear the text as it was originally heard.

Cultural Connotations

Sometimes words or phrases carry cultural connotations that are not readily apparent to the modern reader. For example, in Matthew 9:9–10 Jesus calls Matthew to follow him and then attends a banquet at his home. Consider the beginning of the meal scene in several versions:

"while he was reclining in the house" (closest formal equivalent)
"as Jesus was reclining *at the table* in the house" (NASU)
"While Jesus was having dinner at Matthew's house" (TNIV)
"Matthew invited Jesus and his disciples to be his dinner guests" (NLT)

Which translation is most accurate? The closest formal equivalent, "reclining in the house," leaves out much of the meaning that would have been evident to a first-century reader. The verb "reclining" does not mean simply resting but rather "eating a meal," so the NASU adds that Jesus was reclining *"at the table"* (italics in the NASU are meant to show that these words are not in the Greek).

The posture itself has cultural implications. While common meals were eaten sitting down, "reclining" (on cushions around a low table) normally indicated a more formal banquet or dinner party. The TNIV therefore identifies this as a "dinner at Matthew's house." The NLT goes further, mentioning Matthew's invitation and Jesus and the disciples as "dinner guests." Dinner parties in the ancient world were rituals of social status, and in this passage the Pharisees object because Jesus, a respected rabbi, is dining with despised tax collectors and other sinners (v. 11). In cases like this, translators must decide how much cultural context to provide and how much to leave for the reader to work out.

There are many examples where cultural or religious connotations may not be obvious to the modern reader. In the Gospels evil spirits or demons are sometimes referred to as "unclean spirits" (*akatharta pneumata*; Matt. 10:1; Mark 1:27; 3:11, etc.). "Unclean" in this sense has nothing to do with hygiene. These are not "dirty" demons, but religiously impure or defiled spirit beings standing in opposition to God's purity and holiness. Formal equivalent versions generally retain "unclean spirits"; most functional equivalent versions use "evil spirits." The former risks miscommunication with the modern reader; the latter loses some of the religious context, where ritual purity and defilement were important concerns. Readers can benefit by using both types of versions.

Jews or Jewish Leaders?

The Greek term *Ioudaioi* is notoriously difficult to translate because of its historical, cultural, and social connotations. In the New Testament the word can refer to (1) ethnic Jews, (2) Judeans (i.e., Jews from Judea), or (3) the Jewish religious leaders in Jerusalem.

Especially in the Gospel of John, the term often refers to the religious leaders who opposed Jesus. For example, in John 9:22 the parents of a blind man healed by Jesus are reluctant to acknowledge the healing "because they were afraid of the Jews" (NIV). *Ioudaioi* here obviously refers to the religious leaders, not all Jews (the parents themselves are Jews, as are Jesus and his disciples). The term is translated "Jewish leaders" here and in similar contexts in the NET, TNIV, NLT, and CEV (cf. GNT, NCV; footnotes in HCSB). Of course this issue is particularly sensitive because of the history of anti-Semitism, where passages like this have sometimes been misused to justify violence against Jews.

Three factors further complicate this issue. First, it is not always easy to determine the meaning of the word in each context, and the versions above differ somewhat on when they use "Jews" and when they use "Jewish leaders." Second, there is a sense in which John does hold the Jewish people of Jerusalem responsible for the rejection of the Messiah, since they followed their leaders. While this does not justify using "Jews" in every case, it does complicate its interpretation. Third, John wrote his Gospel at a time when Jews and Christians were increasingly in conflict over their religious differences. Behind the language of "Jesus versus the Jews" in this Gospel is the conflict in John's day between the church and the synagogue.

In light of these complications, the best recourse for translators is to determine on a case-by-case basis the primary sense of the term in each context and to translate accordingly.

Euphemisms

A *euphemism* is an indirect or culturally appropriate way of saying something that might otherwise be viewed as too direct, unpleasant, or offensive. In English we sometimes say that someone "passed away" rather than that he or she "died." "He went to the bathroom" is an American way of saying "he urinated" or "he defecated"; the British say "he went to the toilet." To "make love" or "sleep together" means to have sexual intercourse.

Most cultures use euphemisms. In Hebrew, "to cover your feet" means to go to the bathroom. To "know a woman" is a euphemism for sexual intercourse. The "way of women" (Gen. 31:35; cf. ESV, NRSV, NASU) refers to a woman's monthly period (cf. TNIV, HCSB, NET, NAB, etc.). To "touch a woman" is a Greek euphemism for sexual intercourse (1 Cor. 7:1). To "fall asleep" can mean to die (Acts 13:36; 1 Cor. 12:20; 15:51). Some scholars believe that the "vessel" Paul speaks about in 1 Thessalonians 4:4 is a euphemism for the male sexual organ and so does not refer metaphorically either to a man's "body" (NIV, TNIV, NLT, NJB, ESV) or to his "wife" (NAB, CEV, GNT, GW).

There are three main ways translators can handle euphemisms. They can (1) translate them literally; (2) translate them directly (describe the action without a euphemism); or (3) use a parallel euphemism in the receptor language. This third is usually the best option. The KJV and NJB translate 1 Samuel 24:3 literally, saying Saul went into a cave "to cover his feet." This makes no sense to most readers, so other versions use the English euphemism "to relieve himself" (TNIV, NASU, ESV, NET, NLT, NCV, GW, GNT, CEV). The NKJV has "to attend to his needs" and NAB, "to ease nature."

In Genesis 4:1 some formal equivalent versions retain the euphemism, "Adam knew Eve his wife" (RSV, ESV, NKJV; cf. NRSV). Others translate directly. The NLT reads "had sexual relations with his wife," and GNT, "had intercourse with his wife." Still others use an English euphemism: "made love to" (TNIV, GW); "had relations with" (NASU); "had marital relations with" (NET). The HCSB, trying for the best of both worlds, renders "Adam knew his wife Eve intimately." This doesn't quite work since it is not a common euphemism for sexual relations, implying instead intimate knowledge or an emotional bond.

Some euphemisms carry cultural connotations that translators may want to retain. The Hebrew idiom "to lie down (or 'sleep') with his ancestors" means to die and be buried. Culturally the idiom may go back to the practice whereby a person's body would be allowed to decay in a tomb and then the bones were collected and placed in a common ancestral tomb. It is related to another Hebrew idiom, "gathered to his ancestors," which also means to die (cf. Judg. 2:10; 2 Kings 22:10). In 1 Kings 2:10 the RSV and ESV follow the KJV in translating the first idiom as, "Then David slept with his fathers." This has two problems. First, in English the idiom "slept with" commonly refers to sexual intercourse; second, "fathers" is an archaic way to refer to ancestors.

If the Hebrew idiom "lie down with" (or "sleep with") is a dead metaphor (see chap. 4, pp. 67–69, for this term), then it should be translated simply "David died" or "David died and was buried." GNT says simply, "David died and was buried," and NET, "David passed away" (with a note giving the literal form). If it is a live metaphor, then translators should seek to capture the cultural link to ancestral burial. Notice how various versions handle the euphemism:

"Then David rested with his fathers" (NIV, HCSB, NKJV)
"Then David rested with his ancestors" (TNIV, NAB)
"David lay down in death with his ancestors" (GW)
"Then David died and was buried with his ancestors" (NLT)
"Then David joined his ancestors" (Message)

Weights, Measures, and Money

Certain biblical items are unique to a cultural context and so provide difficulties for translators. This is especially so with weights, measures, and money. Most Bible versions provide a table of biblical weights and measures in an appendix, identifying modern equivalents. But how should these items be translated in the text?

Weights and Measures

For weights and measures, there are two main options for translators: (1) provide a Hebrew or Greek "transliteration" (= spell out the Greek or Hebrew word with English letters), usually with a footnote giving a modern equivalent, or (2) translate using a modern equivalent (sometimes with a footnote giving the Hebrew or Greek transliteration). Consider the difference between the TNIV and the HCSB at 1 Kings 5:11:

"Solomon gave Hiram twenty thousand cors of wheat as food for his household, in addition to twenty thousand baths of pressed olive oil." (TNIV)
"Solomon provided Hiram with 100,000 bushels of wheat as food for his household and 110,000 gallons of beaten oil." (HCSB)

Both provide explanatory footnotes. While the TNIV gives the Hebrew measurements "cors" and "baths" in the text and their modern equivalents in the footnote, the HCSB reverses this. Formal equivalent versions and mediating ones (TNIV, NET, NAB) tend to follow the first option; functional equivalent versions the second. Translators must decide whether they will be culturally more precise (option one) or immediately clear to readers (option two). As with all translation decisions, the goals of accuracy and clarity must be balanced and the target audience kept in mind.

Money

As with weights and measures, words for money can either be transliterated or replaced with modern equivalents. Most formal equivalent and mediating versions transliterate Hebrew and Greek words like shekels, talents, denarii, and minas. Functional equivalent versions occasionally refer to "dollars," but more commonly speak in general terms of silver or gold coins. One exception is that small copper coins like the *kodrantēs, assarion,* and *lepton* (Matt. 5:26; 10:29; Luke 12:59) are identified as "pennies" in most versions (NRSV, ESV, TNIV, NLT, etc.). This works since "penny" has come to mean something of low value in American English ("that's only worth pennies").

The problem with using modern equivalents for money is that its value changes over time. This is particularly evident in the KJV. In Luke 19, the KJV translated Greek *mina* (worth about three month's wages) as a (British) "pound" (worth under two dollars today). Strangely, both the RSV and the NRSV follow the KJV in using "pound," perhaps because of the traditional title, "the parable of the pounds" (Luke 19:11–27). The NKJV and ESV correct this to "minas." Similarly, in Matthew 20:2 the KJV rendered *denarius*—worth a day's wage—as a "penny" (cheap labor indeed!). These examples show the danger of using contemporary units of money that can change drastically over time.

In some cases a third option is to provide the relative value of the money. For example, a denarius in the first century was equivalent to the average wage of a day laborer. In the parable of the workers in the vineyard, most versions translate denarius literally: "He agreed to pay them a denarius for the day" (Matt. 20:2). The NLT, however, reads, "He agreed to pay the normal daily wage," and the CEV "the usual amount for a day's work" (cf. NRSV, GW).

The TNIV does something similar with the talent (*talanton*), a large unit of money worth about six thousand denarii or approximately twenty years' work for a day laborer. In the parable of the unmerciful servant (Matt. 18:23–34), the master forgives his servant an impossibly huge debt of ten thousand talents (200,000 years worth of work!). The servant in turn refuses to forgive his fellow servant a trivial debt of a hundred denarii. Most versions translate literally as ten thousand talents (NIV, NET, HCSB, NRSV, ESV, NASU).

This translation, however, creates two problems. First, if readers do not check the footnotes, they will miss the extreme hyperbole in Jesus' words. "Ten thousand" sounds manageable. Second, the word "talent" today commonly means an "ability" or "gift" (a meaning that arose from Matt. 25:14–30), which could result in misinterpretation for readers. Other versions therefore use a modern equivalent such as "millions of dollars" (NLT, GW, GNT). The TNIV uses "ten thousand bags of gold," since the point is not the precise amount, but the impossibly large contrast between God's forgiveness and our own.

Conclusion

In this chapter we have seen that getting the cultural context right is another challenge translators face. This task is complicated by the fact that different readers come to the text with different levels of knowledge. As a general rule, background material should be supplied by translators (1) when it relates directly to the meaning of the text (without distracting from the main point), (2) when it would have been immediately apparent to the original readers, and (3) when it is likely to be missed by the target audience. The goal, as always, should be to transport readers to the world of the text so that they can understand what was originally heard.

For Further Reading

Beekman, J., and J. Callow. *Translating the Word of God*. Grand Rapids: Zondervan, 1974.

Hill, Harriet. *The Bible at Cultural Crossroads: From Translation to Communication*. Manchester: St. Jerome, 2006.

Nida, Eugene A., and William D. Reyburn. *Meaning across Cultures*. Maryknoll, NY: Orbis, 1981.

Wendland, Ernst R. *The Cultural Factor in Bible Translation*. London: United Bible Societies, 1987.

Chapter 7

Gender and Translation

As we have seen in chapter 3, the meanings of words change over time, and translations must be periodically updated to keep up with these changes. One of the most significant changes in English over the last quarter century has been related to gender language. While it was once commonplace to refer to people as "men" and all fellow Christians as "brothers," such usage has declined significantly in recent years. More inclusive terms like "people" and "brothers and sisters" are used more often today. Bible translators, seeking to stay current with contemporary English, have adapted to these changes. Over the past thirty years, almost every English Bible version either produced or revised has adopted this kind of "gender accurate" language (TNIV, NET, NLT, GW, CEV, NAB, NJB, NRSV, REB, NCV, GNT, NIrV). This is in line with the goal of translating words according to their meaning in context.

Even versions like the ESV and HCSB, which have intentionally reacted against the trend toward gender inclusive language, utilize it far more than their predecessors. A search using Accordance Bible software reveals that the ESV removed the words "man" or "men" 671 times from its predecessor the RSV — clear evidence of the changing state of the English language.

This chapter will examine the benefits and challenges of achieving gender accuracy in Bible translation.

The Nature of Gender Accuracy

While some critics claim that the movement toward gender accurate language is a form of political correctness, the truth is that such language has made our Bible translations more precise and so more accurate. Consider Romans 3:28, which the NIV translated, "For we maintain that a man is justified by faith." The TNIV, its revision, renders the verse, "For we

maintain that a person is justified by faith." Since Paul is obviously referring to people, not just men, the TNIV is more accurate.

The primary meaning of the Greek word *anthrōpos* is "person," not
"man." (We get the English word *anthropology*—the study of human
beings—from this word.) Greek has other words, such as *anēr* ("man")
and *arsēn* ("male"), which more commonly refer to males. Of course the
NIV's translation is not "wrong," since the original translators intended
"man" to be understood generically, that is, referring to people in general. But the English language has changed, and for many readers "man"
now sounds like it refers exclusively to males. The TNIV's "person" is a
double-win for translators. It is both *more clear* and *more accurate*, clarifying the precise meaning of *anthrōpos* in this context.

Biological Gender versus Grammatical Gender

Much of the confusion related to gender accurate language arises from
a misunderstanding of what gender means. In many languages, including Hebrew and Greek, every noun is categorized according to gender.
Hebrew has two genders, masculine and feminine, while Greek has three,
masculine, feminine, and neuter. This is *grammatical* gender, not biological gender (sexual distinction). For example, the Greek word for "sword"
(*machaira*) is feminine, while the word "book" (*biblos*) is masculine. Another word for "book" or "scroll" is *biblion*, which is neuter. There is no
relationship between the nature of the object and its gender.

With reference to persons, grammatical gender usually coincides
with biological gender. The most common Greek word for "man" (*anēr*)
is masculine, while the word for "woman" (*gynē*) is feminine. In other
cases, however, grammatical and biological gender are at odds. The
Greek word for a child (*teknon*) is neuter; yet we do not refer to a child
as "it." In German the word for a young woman is *Mädchen*, a neuter
word.

Nor are generic words always masculine. In Spanish, the word for
"person" is feminine (*la persona*). The same is true in German (*die Person*). In Greek the word is masculine (*anthrōpos*). Does this mean Spanish and German persons are feminine while Greeks are masculine? No,
it means that this is a grammatical category that has nothing to do with
biological gender. Our favorite example is from German, where the word
for "masculinity"—*die Männlichkeit*—is feminine!

Since grammatical gender does not necessarily coincide with biological gender, it is necessary to carefully consider words in context to
determine their meaning. Thousands of examples could be introduced
to show that using inclusive language for masculine generic terms in Hebrew and Greek improves the accuracy of Bible translation. Here are a
few illustrations.

Man or Person?

Older versions of the Bible traditionally translated the Hebrew and Greek words for persons as "man" and "men." Yet as noted above, these words are generic and usually refer both to men and women. Matthew 12:12 in the ESV reads, "Of how much more value is a man [*anthrōpos*] than a sheep!" (cf. HCSB, NASU, NKJV, NIV). Jesus is obviously referring to people here, so the TNIV more accurately renders it, "How much more valuable is a human being than a sheep!" (cf. NLT, NET, NAB, NRSV, GNT, NCV). In Mark 10:26–27 the disciples ask, "Who then can be saved?" In the NIV, Jesus responds, "With man [*anthrōpos*], this is impossible, but not with God." The TNIV recognizes the inclusive nature of *anthrōpos* and translates, "With human beings this is impossible, but not with God" (cf. GNT, NET).

The Hebrew term *ʾadam*, like the Greek *anthrōpos*, usually carries an inclusive sense, referring to both men and women. When in Genesis 6:7 the Lord says, "I will blot out man [*ʾadam*] whom I have created" (NASU; cf. NKJV, ESV, RSV, HCSB), it is both males and females who will be judged. The NLT accurately renders, "I will completely wipe out this human race that I have created" (cf. TNIV, NET, GW, GNT, CEV). The phrase, "Whoever sheds the blood of man [*ʾadam*]" in Genesis 9:6 (ESV) means "whoever sheds human blood" (TNIV; cf. NLT, NRSV, GW).

Brothers or Brothers and Sisters?

The Greek plural noun *adelphoi* can refer to (1) brothers (male siblings); (2) siblings (i.e., brothers and sisters), or (3) people in some other close bond or association. It is sometimes used in the New Testament of physical siblings (see 1 Cor. 9:5), but more often refers figuratively to the kinship between Christian believers.

English versions have traditionally translated the term either as "brothers" or "brethren." The NIV at Philippians 4:1 reads "Therefore, my brothers [*adelphoi*] ... stand firm in the Lord" (cf. ESV, HCSB; "brethren" in KJV, RSV, NKJV, NASU). But in this context, and many others like it, the author is clearly addressing the whole church—both men and women. In the very next verse Paul encourages two women, Euodia and Syntyche, to live in harmony. The TNIV and other versions accurately render *adelphoi* as "Therefore, my brothers and sisters" (cf. NLT, NET, GW, NCV, NRSV). This translation is not a "paraphrase" or a concession to a political correctness. It is exactly what the Greek term meant in its first-century context.

The ESV, while consistently translating the term as "brothers," includes a footnote at its first occurrence in each book acknowledging that it actually means "brothers and sisters":

*Or *brothers and sisters*. The plural Greek word *adelphoi* (translated
"brothers") refers to siblings in a family. In New Testament usage,
depending on the context, *adelphoi* may refer either to men or to
both men and women who are siblings (brothers and sisters) in
God's family, the church.

This footnote reminds us that translation is not about "literally" reproducing words or the form of the text (in this case, a masculine form), but
about accurately reproducing the meaning. The fact that *adelphoi* is one
word in Greek while "brothers and sisters" is three words in English is
irrelevant, so long as the meaning is retained. And the meaning in these
passages is "brothers and sisters" or "fellow believers."

The singular *adelphos* can also be used in a generic sense, meaning
"brother or sister" or "fellow believer." First John 2:9–11 in the NIV
reads, "Anyone who claims to be in the light but hates his brother [*adelphos*] is still in the darkness." Since *adelphos* here clearly refers to a fellow
Christian believer, whether male or female, the NCV translates "brother
or sister." The NLT has "a Christian brother or sister."

Fathers, Forefathers, or Ancestors?

The Greek and Hebrew terms traditionally translated "fathers" (Heb.:
'aboth; Gk.: *pateres*) can refer to actual "fathers" (male parents), to moth-
ers and fathers ("parents"; see Heb. 11:23), or to past generations ("ancestors"; "forefathers"). First Samuel 12:6 reads (TNIV), "It is the LORD
who appointed Moses and Aaron and brought your ancestors [*'aboth*] up
out of Egypt" ("ancestors" also in HCSB, NET, GNT, NLT, GW, NCV,
NJB, NRSV). Since Samuel is speaking of many generations past and
since both men and women came out of Egypt, "ancestors" is the most accurate translation here. The NASU renders the verse "who brought your
fathers up from the land of Egypt" (cf. ESV, NKJV). This is less precise
because it does not clearly refer to generations of long ago and because it
could be read as excluding women.

Care must be taken here, since in some cases "fathers" refers to patriarchal heads of households. For example, Deuteronomy 6:10 (NIV)
reads, "When the LORD your God brings you into the land he swore to
your fathers, to Abraham, Isaac and Jacob, to give you." In such cases,
"ancestors" would not be wrong, since it would include the patriarchs,
but a masculine term like "fathers" or "forefathers" is better since it refers primarily to Abraham, Isaac, and Jacob. The TNIV retains "fathers"
here: "When the LORD your God brings you into the land he swore to
your fathers ..." Of course English still uses "father(s)" to refer to people
of unique significance as founders (e.g., Americans speak of "our found-
ing fathers" and George Washington as the "father of our country"), so

almost all versions retain references to Abraham as the "father of many nations" (Gen. 17:4; Rom. 4:16 – 17; TNIV, NLT, CEV, NCV, NET, etc.). The goal, as always, is to translate words in context with the clearest and most accurate English equivalents available.

Sons, Children, or Descendants?

The most common Hebrew and Greek terms for offspring (Heb.: *banim*; Gk.: *huioi*) can mean different things: "sons," "children," "grandchildren," "descendants," as well appearing in many idioms with a wide range of meanings (e.g., "sons of the prophets"; "sons of the bridechamber"; "sons of light," etc.). Long before the contemporary debate over inclusive language, the KJV often rendered these terms inclusively as "children" rather than "sons." The phrase "children of Israel" occurs 644 times in the KJV. Similarly, in Isaiah 1:2 (KJV), the Lord says of the nation, "I have nourished and brought up children [*banim*], and they have rebelled against me." Matthew 5:44 – 45 in the KJV reads, "Love your enemies ... that ye may be the children [*huioi*] of your Father which is in heaven."

In these and many other contexts, the term clearly refers generically to males and females — "children" rather than "sons." Curiously, while the formal equivalent versions follow the KJV in translating *banim* as "children" in the Old Testament, in the New Testament they often revert back to "sons" (see Matt. 5:45 NKJV, NASU, RSV, ESV).

These examples represent the tip of the iceberg. Thousands of passages could be cited from both the Old and New Testaments to show that gender accurate language more precisely represents the meaning of the original text.

Some Clarifications

Several clarifications are in order. First, as the example of "fathers" above shows, we are not advocating the blanket replacement of masculine terms with inclusive language. This not about gender "neutrality" (as some have claimed), but about gender "accuracy." The goal is not to eliminate gender distinctions in Scripture, but to clarify them. Passages that refer exclusively to males should remain masculine, and references to females should remain feminine. But when the context indicates that both males and females are in view, inclusive terms like "person," "brothers and sisters," "children," and "ancestors" are more precise and so more accurate. This is simply good translation policy.

Another clarification concerns language related to God. Some people have expressed fears that the use of gender accurate language is a "slippery slope" leading to the identification of God as "she" or as "our Mother in heaven." But this is an unnecessary concern, since such changes would be contrary to the goal of gender accuracy, which is to capture as precisely as possible the original meaning of the text.

Two points must be kept in mind concerning God-language. (1) God is neither male nor female. He is pure spirit (John 1:18; 4:24). Numbers 23:19 reads, "God is not a man [i.e., a human being], that he should lie, nor a son of man, that he should change his mind" (NIV; cf. Hos. 11:9; Job 9:32). (2) Although some of the biblical images related to God are feminine (e.g., God is like a mother who comforts her children: Ps. 131:2; Isa. 46:3; 49:15; 66:13; Hos. 11:3–4), most are masculine. God is King of the universe, sovereign Lord of all, and Father to his people as their Creator and Redeemer (Deut. 32:18; Ps. 103:13; Hos. 11:1). Jesus calls God his Father (Mark 14:36) and invites his disciples to pray to him as "our Father in heaven" (Matt. 6:9). It is appropriate, then, to refer to God as "he"—not because God is a male, but because he is a person, and because a masculine pronoun more accurately reflects the biblical metaphors like "Father" used to describe God.

None of the versions discussed in this chapter introduce feminine language for God or eliminate masculine pronouns or metaphors used for him. There are indeed a few feminist versions that do so, such as *The New Testament and Psalms: An Inclusive Version* (1995) and *The Inclusive Bible* (2007) produced by Priests for Equality. But these versions have a very different agenda, seeking to eliminate patriarchal references from the Bible. This is a completely different goal from gender accuracy, which is to reflect as accurately as possible the original meaning of the text. Gender accurate versions seek to introduce inclusive language only with reference to human beings and only when the original meaning included both sexes.

Some Difficult Issues

Ambiguous Passages

In some passages it is difficult to determine whether the reference is to men only or to both men and women. In such cases translators must make a decision based on a careful examination of the context. While the Greek noun *anēr* (plural: *andres*) normally means "man," in some contexts it may refer to people in general. For example, in Matthew 12:41 Jesus says, "The men [*andres*] of Nineveh will stand up at the judgment with this generation and condemn it" (NIV; cf. RSV, NASU, HCSB). Since females were among those converted at Nineveh, the sense here seems to be "people" (TNIV, NET, NLT, GNT, CEV, NCV, NRSV).

Similarly, in Matthew 14:35 was it the "people" (NLT, NET, NRSV, GNT, CEV, NJB) of Gennesaret or the "men" (TNIV, GW, NIV) who brought their sick to Jesus? The letter of James also seems to use *anēr* in an inclusive sense. James 1:12 reads, "Blessed is the man [*anēr*] who perseveres under trial" (NIV). Does this mean "man" or "person"? NRSV says, "Blessed is anyone who endures temptation." In 1:20 James says that "man's anger [*orgē andros*] does not bring about the righteous life God desires" (NIV). It seems clear that this is human anger, so the NLT translates, "Human anger does not produce the righteousness God desires" (cf. James 3:2).

Like *anēr*, the Hebrew term *ᵓish* can mean either "man" or "person" depending on the context. In Exodus 32:28, did three thousand "men" (NASU, ESV, HCSB, NJB, GNT, CEV) or "people" (NAB, NIV, TNIV, NET, NLT, GW) die in the plague following the golden calf incident? Similarly, did the judgment for David's census in 2 Samuel 24:15 result in the death of seventy thousand "men" (NKJV, HCSB) or "people" (ESV, NASU, NIV, TNIV)? In Exodus 33:8, 10, was it the "men" (RSV, NKJV) or the "people" (NIV, TNIV, NET, HCSB, NASU, ESV) who stood at the entrance of their tents when Moses entered the Tent of Meeting? Notice that in these examples even the "literal" versions are divided. When the context is ambiguous, translators must make difficult decisions based on the available evidence.

Resumptive Masculine Pronouns

One of the most difficult and complex issues related to gender language involves *resumptive masculine pronouns*. These are pronouns that follow an indefinite noun or pronoun and refer back to it. Consider the following sentence: "If anyone keeps my word, he will never see death" (John 8:51 NIV). Although the word "anyone" is generic, referring to either men or women, the resumptive pronoun "he" is masculine. Ideally, it should be neutral to agree with its antecedent "anyone." But English does not have an inclusive third person singular pronoun ("it" only works for things, not for people). Using "he or she" can be awkward and cumbersome.

There are several ways to translate the sentence:

1. Use a masculine pronoun (as above): "If anyone keeps my word, he will not see death."
2. Pluralize the construction: "Those who keep my word will not see death."
3. Use a singular "they": "If anyone keeps my word, they will not see death."
4. Use a second person: "If you keep my word you will not see death."
5. Use a noun instead of a pronoun: "If anyone keeps my word, that person will not see death."

6. Modify the construction to eliminate the pronoun: "Whoever keeps my word will not see death."

All of these represent accurate translations, since they all express the generic meaning that *a person* who follows Jesus' message will not experience spiritual death. Yet all also have some inconsistency. Option 1 is inconsistent concerning *gender*, since a masculine pronoun in English is being used for an inclusive reference in Greek (*tis*, "anyone"). Options 2 and 3 are inconsistent concerning *number*, since a plural construction is used for an indefinite antecedent. Option 4 is inconsistent concerning *person*, since a second person ("you") is used for a third. Option 5 quickly becomes stylistically awkward, since repeating a noun over and over again can become cumbersome. Option 6 changes the construction from a conditional clause to an indefinite one.

There is no perfect solution and translators must make difficult choices. Some opponents of inclusive language claim that only the first option is accurate, since it is the most "literal." But this is not actually true. In the Greek sentence of John 8:51, there is no masculine pronoun "he." The verb "will see" is in the third person singular (he, she, it), but verbs in Greek do not specify gender. Even if a masculine pronoun were present, it would not mean "he," since pronouns get their meaning from the noun or pronoun they replace, in this case "anyone."

The important thing to remember is that the *meaning*, not the form, must be retained in translation. Using a second person ("you"—option 4) works in the example above because in English we often use "you" in generic sentences. The proverb, "You get what you pay for" means "A person gets what he (or she) pays for." Some English stylists consider singular "they" (option 3) to be ungrammatical and warn against its use. Increasingly, however, stylists and English handbooks accept it as legitimate and point to its long and venerable history in the English language, going back as far as Geoffrey Chaucer and appearing in great writers like William Shakespeare, Jane Austen, and George Bernard Shaw.

Even the KJV sometimes uses the singular "they" (Matt. 18:35). Most English speakers today would find it awkward to say, "Everybody likes ice cream, doesn't he?" even though that is grammatically "correct" (according to some grammarians). Instead most people would say: "Everybody likes ice cream, don't they?" This is a singular "they." In light of its long history in the English language and growing acceptance as standard English, contemporary English Bible versions have begun to use it more often.

Pluralizing the whole sentence (option 2) also works in generic contexts because generics are *notionally* plural, meaning they refer to people (note the plural) in general: "Those who work hard will succeed" means the same as "A person who works hard will succeed." Only a wooden literalist would claim that the first sentence means "groups" who work hard will succeed. Any ordinary English reader immediately recognizes that "those" means "those individuals" in generic contexts like this.

Evidence that pluralizing does not necessarily distort the meaning of the text comes from the Bible itself, since biblical writers sometimes translate masculine singular generics with plural constructions. Consider these examples, where the apostle Paul quotes from the Old Testament:

Old Testament Text	Paul's New Testament Citation
Isa. 52:7: How lovely on the mountains are the feet of *him* who brings good news.	Rom. 10:15b: ... As it is written, "How beautiful are the feet of *those* who bring good news!"
Ps. 36:1b: There is no fear of God before *his* eyes.	Rom. 3:10, 18: As it is written ... "There is no fear of God before *their* eyes."
Ps. 32:1: Blessed is *he* whose transgressions are forgiven, whose sins are covered.	Rom. 4:6–7: David says the same thing ... "Blessed are *they* whose transgressions are forgiven, whose sins are covered."

In all three cases Paul translated Hebrew singulars with Greek plurals. He clearly recognized that generic plurals in Greek accurately represent the meaning of generic singulars in Hebrew. He changed the form but retained the meaning.

The Humanity of Jesus Christ

Jesus Christ was certainly a man (a male human being), and any attempts to remove masculine language related to him should be avoided. There are cases, however, when a passage is not about Jesus' maleness but about his humanity. In 1 Timothy 2:5, for example, the NIV reads, "For there is one God and one mediator between God and men, the man Christ Jesus." The point is that Jesus is able to save human beings (not just "men"!) because he himself is human. The TNIV more accurately renders the verse, "For there is one God and one mediator between God and human beings, Christ Jesus, himself human." See also Philippians 2:8, where Jesus "was found in appearance as a human being" (TNIV).

While 1 Timothy 2:5 is straightforward, other passages are more difficult. In 1 Corinthians 15 and Romans 5, Paul draws an analogy between Adam and Jesus. First Corinthians 15:21 reads: "For since death came through a man, the resurrection of the dead comes also through a man." The TNIV reads, "For since death came through a human being, the resurrection of the dead comes also through a human being." This passage raises difficult theological questions. Is Paul's primary point that because humans sinned, a human being must be the agent of salvation? Or is it—as some have claimed—that Adam serves as the (male) representative head of the human race? Those with different views on Federal theology (where Adam serves as representative of humanity) will likely come to different conclusions. While translators can never be completely objective, it is important to seek Paul's meaning in context and to translate accordingly.

Messianic Passages

It has sometimes been argued that pluralizing distorts the meaning of Old Testament messianic texts. In Psalm 8:4 the NIV reads, "What is man ['enosh] that you are mindful of him, the son of man [ben 'adam] that you care for him?" Both 'enosh and ben 'adam are references to human beings in general, so the TNIV translates, "What are mere mortals that you are mindful of them, human beings that you care for them?" (cf. NET, NRSV, NJB, NAB, NCV, NLT, GNT, CEV). Does pluralizing the construction blur the application of this psalm to Jesus in Hebrews 2:6?

To address this issue, we must consider the meaning of the psalm both in its Old Testament context and in its application to Jesus in Hebrews 2. It can hardly be denied that the psalmist is speaking inclusively rather than exclusively in Psalm 8. He does not mean, "What are males ..." but rather "What are human beings ..." All commentators agree that 'enosh and ben 'adam are generic references to humanity.

Most commentators also agree that this same meaning applies to the use of the psalm in Hebrews 2:6–8. The author is not claiming that the psalm refers exclusively to Christ, but that the *destiny of humanity* as expressed in the psalm ("to be crowned with glory and honor," vv. 6–8) has been fulfilled in Christ (v. 9). The reference to "him" in verse 8 is not to Jesus but to humankind. Though man's (= humanity's) original destiny was to be crowned with glory and honor and for creation to be subject to him (see Gen. 1:28), "at present we do not see everything subject to him." In its present fallen state, humanity has not achieved its true destiny.

Jesus, however, through his suffering and death has fulfilled the ultimate destiny of humanity by being made for a time "a little lower than the angels," but now "crowned with glory and honor" (vv. 7, 9). William Lane sums up well: "In Jesus we see exhibited humanity's true vocation. In an extraordinary way he fulfills God's design for all creation and displays what had always been intended for all humankind, according to Ps 8."[1] Psalm 8, both in its Old Testament context and in its context in Hebrews, is about God's intention for *humanity*. Jesus fulfills this destiny by acting as the true human representative. The plural references in both Psalm 8:4 and Hebrews 2:6–8 capture this sense well.

Another Old Testament messianic passage where pluralizing has been criticized for blurring a messianic reference is in Psalm 34:20. Compare the RSV of verses 19–20 with the NRSV:

> RSV: "Many are the afflictions of the righteous; but the LORD delivers him out of them all. He keeps all his bones; not one of them is broken."
>
> NRSV: "Many are the afflictions of the righteous, but the LORD rescues them from them all. He keeps all their bones; not one of them will be broken."

The TNIV, NLT, GNT, CEV, NJB, and NAB also introduce plural references. Some critics have claimed that pluralizing the sentence distorts the messianic application to Jesus in John 19:36, where Jesus fulfills the prophecy that "not one of his bones will be broken" (NIV).

Several comments are in order. First, it is not certain that John 19:36 is referring to Psalm 34:20. Many commentators see instead a Passover lamb allusion drawn from Exodus 12:46 and Numbers 9:12. Even if we assume for the sake of argument that Psalm 34:20 is in view, the psalm is fulfilled typologically, rather than uniquely, by Christ. Verse 18 of the psalm reads: "The LORD is close to the brokenhearted and saves those who are crushed in spirit" (NIV). In the Hebrew text both "brokenhearted" and "those who are crushed" are plurals, indicating that the singulars in verses 19–20 are also generic, referring to righteous sufferers in general. The translators of the Septuagint (the Greek Old Testament) understood it this way, since they translated using plurals throughout. In its original context, then, this is a psalm of righteous sufferers, who persevere in their faith in God. Jesus dies as the righteous sufferer par excellence.

Conclusion

This chapter has demonstrated that the use of gender accurate language can significantly improve the reliability of a translation. Terms like "person," "brothers and sisters," "children," and "ancestors" are more specific than their masculine generic counterparts and so more accurate. Inclusive language, however, should be introduced only when the original meaning of the text included both males and females.

For Further Reading

Carson, D. A. *The Inclusive Language Debate: A Plea for Realism.* Grand
    Rapids: Baker, 1998.
Strauss, Mark L. *Distorting Scripture? The Challenge of Bible Translation
    and Gender Accuracy.* Downers Grove, IL: InterVarsity Press, 1998.
(For a contrary view:)
Poythress, Vern S., and Wayne A. Grudem. *The Gender-Neutral Bible
    Controversy: Muting the Masculinity of God's Words.* Nashville: Broad-
    man & Holman, 2000.

Part 4

Other Translation Issues: Text and Presentation

Chapter 8

The Question of the Original Text

O ne might well assume that the first task of translators is to determine the *meaning* of the words in the original language, so that they can be transferred into words with comparable meaning in the receptor language. But in fact the first task is to know *which* words are to be translated. Before the invention of the printing press, all documents were hand-copied by copyists or "scribes." A hand-copied document is known as a "manuscript" (meaning "written by hand"). Since such copying inevitably resulted in errors, the translators' *first task* is to be sure that the words being translated are the words that the original authors actually wrote.

It is of some historical interest in this regard that when the Revised Standard Version (RSV) was published in 1952, it set off an enormous storm of protest. While this antagonism focused in part on some questionable renditions, such as "young woman" for "virgin" in Isaiah 7:14, the major point of contention had to do with "all the words they left out of the Bible." But did the RSV translators "leave words out," or had the KJV included extra words—hundreds of words—that were not a part of the original biblical writings? The answer to these questions has to do with the historical discipline known as *textual criticism*. By definition this is the scholarly discipline that sorts through the manuscript evidence for the Bible and tries to determine on scientific grounds which readings (or "variants") are most likely to be original.

The Need for Textual Criticism

The need for textual criticism differs between the Old Testament and the New, mostly because of the two considerably different ways handwritten copies of the two were transmitted in antiquity. The Hebrew Bible as it has come down to us had a long history of hand-copying within a carefully controlled environment, which Old Testament scholars generally consider to be one of great care. The "standard" Hebrew text is the Masoretic Text, named after the Jewish scribes known as the Masoretes, who meticulously copied it. The best evidence for the accuracy of the Masoretic text comes from a magnificent scroll of Isaiah, one of the Dead Sea Scrolls discovered near Khirbet Qumran in Israel in the late 1940s. The Isaiah scroll, which preceded the earliest known Hebrew manuscript by nearly ten centuries, turned out to have a Hebrew text that, given the time distance between them, was remarkably similar to the traditional (Masoretic) text.

But this is only part of the story of the Old Testament text. Old Testament textual critics compare the Masoretic Text not only with copies of the Hebrew Bible found in the Dead Sea Scrolls, but also with other ancient texts, such as the Samaritan Pentateuch and the Greek Old Testament known as the Septuagint (abbreviated LXX). The Septuagint is particularly important in this regard. As early as three hundred years before Christ, the Hebrew Bible had been translated into Greek for Jews in the Diaspora (i.e., those living outside of Palestine) whose only language was Greek. The Septuagint was in fact the only version available to the majority of the people who first received the documents that became our New Testament.

Because of the antiquity of the Septuagint, translators will occasionally follow its readings over those of the Masoretic Text. This is especially so when a reading from the Septuagint agrees with one found in the Dead Sea Scrolls. These cases are exceptional, however, and the Masoretic text is generally considered highly reliable. All contemporary English versions use it as their primary source text for the Old Testament. The standard edition used in colleges, universities, and seminaries is the *Biblia Hebraica Stuttgartensia* (5th edition).

The copying history (transmission) of the New Testament is considerably more complex; and since most of the difficulties people have regarding the original text of the Bible are found in the New Testament, we will illustrate the problems faced by translators from this part of the Bible. First, a few words about the "need" and the "sources" for the task at hand.

The *need* for textual criticism can be found in the fact that for the New Testament we are aware of approximately 5,400 handwritten copies (manuscripts) in Greek alone. These include copies of the whole New Testament, shorter collections of books (such as the Gospels or the Pauline letters), single books, and even very small fragments of only a sentence or two. A few of these latter (single books and fragments) date from as early as the second century AD, while the great majority of the former date from a much later period (from the years 1000 to 1540). Although these diverse manuscripts are found in libraries all over the world, they have all been named and numbered, and many of them are available to be viewed by whoever might be interested.

Important for our present discussion is the fact that there are *no two manuscripts* of the New Testament that are exactly alike—even when we know that one of them is a copy of the other. The reason is that copyists made mistakes, mostly careless, but sometimes deliberate, as they tried to clarify or harmonize to a companion passage the sacred text they were copying.

Here is a case, then, where quantity counts for very little, and quality (and age) count for everything. Indeed, the great majority of manuscripts (known collectively as the Majority Text) reflect an accumulation of centuries of copying errors, which have made their way into these later manuscripts. So the greater value lies with the manuscripts that are demonstrably earlier; and this is especially so when the same reading is found in a cross-section of early witnesses that are widely dispersed geographically. For example, when a reading (variant) is found in early manuscripts that come from the western part of the Roman empire as well as early manuscripts that come from the eastern churches, we can assume that both readings independently go back to an even earlier common source.

The science and art of textual criticism is a highly developed discipline. In addition to evaluating the age and geographical dispersion of manuscripts ("external evidence"), textual critics have developed principles for evaluating variant readings among manuscripts ("internal evidence") to identify and eliminate copyist errors. The net result is that there is near unanimous agreement among biblical scholars that the Greek text used to translate our contemporary English versions is very close to the original text of the New Testament. In the small percentage of passages that remain uncertain, one can be sure that the original is either in the text or is the alternative found in the footnote. So at this point the modern reader is well served.

The only contemporary translation that differs in this matter is the New King James Version (NKJV), a modern revision of the King James Version (KJV). The KJV and the NKJV were both translated from the Greek text known as the Textus Receptus ("Received Text"), which was compiled using a small number of very late manuscripts available to the KJV translators in the early 1600s. The Textus Receptus agrees in most cases with the Majority Text (the text reflecting the majority of manuscripts—most of which are also very late).

While readers should be aware of this significant deficiency in both the KJV and the NKJV, we hasten to add that the sum total of manuscript differences still make up a relatively small percentage of the biblical text and seldom affect important points of doctrine. Furthermore, the NKJV includes footnotes that provide variant readings from both the Majority

Text and the critical text (see next paragraph). Readers of the NKJV should therefore be cautioned that the original reading more often appears in its footnotes than in its text.

In contrast to the KJV and NKJV, all other modern versions follow the critical text. *Critical* is not a negative term but simply denotes the Greek text achieved by using the method of textual *criticism* to identify and eliminate copyist errors. Critical texts also provide footnotes identifying variant readings and their manuscript support so that students who know Greek can evaluate variants for themselves. The standard critical editions of the Greek New Testament are the Nestle-Aland 27th edition (NA[27]) and the United Bible Societies' 4th edition (USB[4]). These two contain essentially the same Greek text, with only minor differences of format and punctuation. Both editions note variant readings in their "apparatus" (footnotes), although Nestle-Aland lists many more variants. The UBS text was especially designed for translators and so includes only variants that are significant for the interpretation and translation of the text.

In summary, because of the wealth of manuscript evidence for both the Old and New Testaments and the reliable methods of textual criticism, readers of the English Bible can be confident that behind their translation lies a Hebrew and Greek text close to what the original authors actually wrote.

Some Illustrations of Textual Differences in English Translations

The great majority of differences among the Greek manuscripts of the New Testament are of three basic kinds:

1. A letter, word, or words have been either *added* to or *omitted* from the original text.
2. A word or words have been *substituted* for those in the original text.
3. A word or words (sentences only rarely) have been *transposed*, either in immediate proximity or to different places in a sentence or clause.

Most translational difficulties occur in the first and second categories, places where the actual wording of the manuscripts differ—because one word has been substituted for another, or because a letter or word or phrase has been added (usually) or omitted (less frequently) by the scribes copying manuscripts. The reason for the greater frequency of addition over omission is that omission is usually accidental, while addition requires at least some awareness on the part of the scribe. Sometimes scribes tried to "help out" an author by clarifying what was unclear or by "correcting" what appeared to them to be difficult. The majority of such "corrections" and clarifications took the form of adding words or rearranging them. Rarely did scribes deliberately omit words from the sacred text they were copying.

In what follows we offer several types of variants that made their way into the manuscript tradition.

Harmonization

One of the more common adjustments to the text was the scribal tendency to harmonize passages. Harmonization sometimes occurred within a given passage, sometimes with the wording of similar passages, and especially between similar passages or sayings of Jesus among the Synoptic Gospels (Matthew, Mark, Luke). One may assume that scribes more often conformed passages to one another than *dis*harmonized them, and therefore a harmonized reading is usually not the original reading.

We begin with an example that is not found in the majority of manuscripts (the Majority Text) and thus is not in the KJV, but which illustrates a common phenomenon. Matthew's version of Peter's confession (Matt. 16:16) reads, "You are the Christ, the Son of the living God," while Mark has only, "You are the Christ" (8:29) and Luke has, "[You are] the Christ of God" (9:20). Given Matthew's pride of place in the canon, it comes as no surprise that later scribes conformed both Mark and Luke to Matthew's version.

A similar harmonization that did make its way into the majority of later manuscripts is Luke's version of the cry of the demon, "[You are] the Son of God!" (Luke 4:41). This was frequently conformed to Matthew 16:16, so that in the KJV (cf. NKJV) Luke 4:41 reads, "Thou art Christ the Son of God."

Such harmonizations happen in Paul's letters as well, but much less frequently. This can be illustrated from the opening words in his two Thessalonian letters. In the first letter, his salutation reads simply: "Grace to you and peace." In the second letter Paul added the source of such grace and peace: "from God the Father and the Lord Jesus Christ." Since some form of this phrase occurs in the salutation of all the rest of Paul's preserved letters, it is not surprising that by the fourth century scribes began to add it in 1 Thessalonians 1:1 as well. The fact that the earliest and best copies, both East and West, do not have these words makes it certain that they did not originate with Paul but with some later scribes. The words are found in the KJV and the NKJV, but not in other contemporary versions.

The reality of harmonization among manuscripts is one of the two primary reasons (along with the problem of archaic language) for people to choose something other than the KJV as their primary Bible. By every criterion of historical probability, copyists did not deliberately *dis*harmonize the Gospel records. Rather, familiarity with these texts often caused these scribes to bring the first three Gospels into conformity with one another.

Conformity

Closely related to the scribal tendency to harmonize passages was a tendency to conform passages to more common expressions. For example, in 2 Thessalonians 3:3 Paul tells the Thessalonian believers that "the Lord is faithful," referring clearly to Christ, who had just been called "the Lord" in two preceding sentences (2:16 and 3:1). But because Paul more often ascribes faithfulness to God the Father (e.g., 1 Cor. 1:9; 10:13, etc.), many early scribes changed the passage to "God is faithful," a reading still found in the Latin Bible. Since in the Greek text the word "faithful" comes first in Paul's sentence ("faithful is the Lord"), here is a simple case of later scribes anticipating the familiar ("God") and changing it accordingly.

The same thing happens to Paul's use of the apostle Peter's Aramaic name, Kephas (traditionally, Cephas), which occurs four times in both 1 Corinthians and Galatians. For reasons that are not certain, scribes kept the Aramaic name in its occurrences in 1 Corinthians. In the four instances in Galatians, however, they regularly changed it to "Peter," three of which eventually found their way into the Majority Text (1:18; 2:11, 14). Thus only in 2:9, where the threesome of James, Kephas, and John are mentioned together, does "Cephas" make the KJV. That scribes would have gone the other way—changing the well-known Greek name "Peter" to the Aramaic "Kephas"—would be nearly impossible to account for.

Clarification

Although the phenomenon of clarification does not occur as often as one might expect, there are enough examples to suggest that later scribes were interested in making the Bible understandable to their church. In a few instances they removed what might have appeared to them to be mistakes on the part of either the inspired author or of a copyist before them.

Thus in Mark 1:2, according to the better early manuscripts, Mark referred to "what was written in Isaiah the prophet," but then he begins the citation with words from Malachi 3:1. Later scribes clarified this by changing "Isaiah the prophet" to "the prophets." Another way of eliminating what scribes perceived as a problem in the text can be found in 1 Thessalonians 3:2, whose difficult genitive we noted above (pp. 79–80). The majority of manuscripts got out of the difficulty of Paul's appearing to have called Timothy "God's co-worker" by adding another noun between "brother" and "co-worker." So instead of "our brother and co-worker of God," the majority of manuscripts read "our brother, God's servant, and our co-worker." Since something similar to this was certainly Paul's intent, scribes "helped Paul out" by adding a second noun and letting the genitive "of God" modify that noun.

A similar kind of "addition" can be found in several manuscripts of Acts, so that Acts 15:33 is followed by a verse 34, which Luke himself did not write. The addition reads, "however, it seemed good to Silas to remain there." Some scribe added these words so that Silas would still be in Antioch in verse 40, when Paul "chose Silas and departed." Although this verse 34 is found in only a small number of manuscripts, one of these happened to serve as the basis of the Textus Receptus on which the KJV was based; and that is how it got its number.

Another example of a scribe "helping the author out" can be found in John 6:11. In John's somewhat abbreviated narrative, he says that "after giving thanks, Jesus distributed the loaves to those who were seated." After the word "distributed" some early scribes added that he gave the bread "to the disciples, and the disciples to those who were seated"—which according to the Synoptic Gospels is what happened, but was simply not mentioned by John.

A final example of clarification of yet another kind, which affects nothing but Greek grammar, can be found in 2 Corinthians 3:17, where Paul says simply, and without verbs, "where the Spirit of the Lord, freedom." A scribe (or scribes) added "there" before freedom, to turn the sentence into more normal Greek (= "where ... there"). And for the sake of English, translators must also add the verb "is" to the sentence. There are many examples of this kind in the manuscript tradition of the New Testament, but they seldom affect our English translations, which must add the words, in any case, in order to make sense of Paul's abbreviated Greek.

Theologically Motivated Changes

Here we offer two examples from among the many that could be assigned to this category. The first one, from 1 Corinthians 6:20, is probably the result of the ascetic worldview that emerged in the church in the third and fourth centuries. At this point in the letter Paul has been arguing against the practice of Corinthian men going to prostitutes, which they apparently justified with the belief that what happened in the body did not really affect one's spiritual nature. At the end of his argument, Paul concludes: "therefore honor God with your bodies" (TNIV). By the fourth century scribes had added: "and with your spirit, which belongs to God." It is not that this is untrue; rather it is irrelevant to the present argument, which has to do with men using their bodies for sexually immoral purposes.

Similarly, in John 7:39, John interprets something Jesus had just said in verse 37. John explains that what Jesus said was pointing to the future coming of the Spirit. But John concluded with the abbreviated clause, "for the Spirit was not yet." Since this could be understood to mean that the Spirit did not yet exist, early scribes, besides often adding the word "Holy" to "Spirit," made two independent changes to make sure John was not misunderstood. One set of manuscripts has, "the Spirit was not yet on them," while others have, "the Spirit had not yet been given." It should be noted that most English translations, including formal equivalent ones, have done the same thing, translating John's abbreviated phrase idiomatically as "for the Spirit was not yet given" (NASB, NASU; cf. RSV, ESV; but see NRSV: "for as yet there was no Spirit").

Conclusion

Biblical translation involves the transfer of the meaning of words originally written in Hebrew, Aramaic, and Greek into functionally equivalent words in English. But because the Bible was transmitted for centuries by handwritten copies (manuscripts), the first task of the translator is to determine *which* words are to be put into English when there are differences in these copies.

For Further Reading

Metzger, Bruce. *The Text of the New Testament: Its Transmission, Corruption and Restoration.* 3rd ed. New York & Oxford: Oxford University Press, 1992.
Tov, Emmanuel. *Textual Criticism of the Hebrew Bible.* 2nd ed. Minneapolis: Fortress, 2001.

Chapter 9

Issues of Style and Format

Throughout most of this book we have examined translation topics related to the *meaning* of the text of Scripture. In this chapter we survey a variety of other decisions translators must make, including issues of style, reading level, format, and presentation.

Style and Reading Level

A primary concern facing biblical translators is the "reading level" of the English that will go into the translation. Historically, most translators of the English Bible have been biblical scholars, who sometimes instinctively use language that is not easily understood by ordinary readers. This means that the first, and most critical, decision made by translators, either as individuals or as a team, has to do with the audience intended for their translation. In general, functional equivalent versions like the CEV, GNT, NLT, NCV, and GW are more sensitive to audience reading level than their formal equivalent counterparts. This is because, by design, functional equivalence seeks language that is natural and idiomatic in the receptor language.

Establishing a version's reading level calls for a careful consideration of several matters: the choice of words, whether they will be more common or more literary; the length of words, whether to limit the number of syllables in a word; the length of sentences; and the end product, whether it will be useful for people who speak English as a second language. Translators should also keep in mind that much of the New Testament was written in *koinē* (i.e., common or everyday) Greek rather than a more highly literary Greek (Luke-Acts and Hebrews are the two most notable exceptions).

The first matter, then, always has to do with the choice of words, whether they will be more common or more literary. That is, *what* English is to be used in the translation, that of the scholar or of the layperson? And if the latter, the question is still *which* layperson—the "college educated" or the (more mythical) "person on the street." The fact is that good English can, and should, speak clearly to both groups.

What one must avoid is "sesquipedalian grandiloquence." For example, we can say both "work" or "labor," and thus "hard work" or "laborious," since both communicate the same thing. But "hard work" probably speaks to a wider range of people. Or, as we have just done, the translator can say either "speak to" or "communicate"; again both are understandable to native English speakers, but what, for example, about readers for whom English is a second language? A good translation should probably aim to err on the side of shorter words, but do so without giving up either good English style or meaning. After all, in some cases a longer word is either the best choice or the only one that captures the sense of the Greek or Hebrew.

A good illustration of this is the Greek word *lēstēs*, which is used by the Gospel writers to describe the two who were crucified with Jesus. While the word can mean simply "robber" or "bandit," its meaning was also extended to refer to those who robbed and vandalized in the context of trying to unsettle things in Palestine with the ultimate aim of overthrowing Roman rule. The context in this case, especially the fact that Barabbas was well known to the crowds, suggests that the two who were crucified were not simply "thieves" or "robbers," but were brigands whose ultimate aim was insurrection.

So what is the best word in *English* to describe Barabbas and his companions? Probably "insurrectionist"; but will that be understood by all? "Robbers," on the other hand, is too narrow to catch the point. The TNIV settled on "rebels," which, while not precise, moves in the right direction. The NLT and the NAB have "revolutionaries," which also captures the sense well with language that most people will understand, as perhaps "terrorist" might in some sectors today.

The matter of sentence length is also an important consideration. This, in fact, is one of the standard means of measuring the reading level of any work in English. The "math" here is quite simple: the longer the sentences, the less accessible the work is to younger and second-language readers. Functional equivalent versions tend to break long Greek sentences into shorter English ones for clarity and readability. Formal equivalent versions try to keep the Greek sentence intact. Mediating versions usually find some compromise between these two.

It is interesting to note that when the NIV, a mediating version, appeared, it was criticized by some scholars in this regard. By shortening the sentences, the translators also tended to leave out many of the "connecting signals" (especially conjunctions) that teachers and preachers find useful to show students and congregations how one sentence is related to another. This was especially true of Paul's frequent use of *gar* ("for"), a Greek conjunction that connects many of his clauses, especially in argumentation. The NIV translators argued that the frequent repetition of "for" created awkward and unnatural English, and that the connection between clauses was clear from the context itself. In the majority of cases, this was certainly true, although the connection is certainly *more* obvious when *gar* is translated. Here we have a tension between natural, idiomatic English and a more precise translation. It was for this reason—the quest for greater precision—that some of these conjunctions were restored in the TNIV.

The matter of style and reading level can be illustrated by a "tale of two Bibles," the New English Bible (1961 NT; 1970) and the New International Version (1973 NT; 1978). The titles themselves tell some of the story. The "English" in the NEB was first of all aimed toward readers in Great Britain; but even there its usefulness was limited, since it had been set at such a high reading level of English (British academic). The result was that it never did catch on with the ordinary believer in the pew, even in Great Britain.

The translators of the NIV, on the other hand, took the word "international" seriously, even though they were well along in the process before the name was chosen. Their stated aim was twofold: first, to offer a wholly new translation of the Bible into English for use both by individuals and in the church. Second, they deliberately set the reading level so that it would be useful for second-language people. Their measure of success is indicated by the fact that of all the translations since the KJV, the NIV has been the best-selling Bible in North America and beyond for over two decades.

The issue of intended readership is so important that people would benefit from reading the preface to their translation. This will make them aware of the version's intended audience as well as other important matters related to the translation process.

Paragraphs, Chapters, and Verses

One of the major difficulties facing all Bible translators is how to properly mark "sense units," especially sentences and paragraphs. While such sense units existed in biblical Greek and Hebrew, they were not marked with punctuation. For the sake of the reader, one of the tasks of the translator is to identify such units.

Probably through the influence of Latin, two things came to exist in English that did not exist in Greek antiquity: the separation of words with a space between them, and the marking of sense units by various kinds of punctuation. Since the object of translation is to transfer *meaning* from one language to the other, one of the tasks of translators is to identify these units in the original language and punctuate them accordingly in English.

Our earliest New Testament manuscripts were written in a script similar to our capital letters, known as "uncial" script, and with no spacing between the words. This phenomenon carried on well into the fourth century. For the most part scribes showed a degree of sensitivity in breaking words at syllables at the end of a line, but this was not always the case. So, for example, the scribe of a manuscript known as P[66], a copy of the Gospel of John that dates from the late second or early third century, was quite relaxed on this matter (just as he also was with spelling). He would often end a line of text with just a single letter from the next word. In so doing, of course, he was able to keep his margins straight!

Putting the Greek text into English, however, requires that it be *English*, and therefore that there be sentences with proper punctuation. Thus English statements must end with a period, questions with a question mark, and what is understood to be exclamatory with an exclamation point. All of this, of course, involves *interpretation*. But, as we have seen throughout this book, every aspect of translation involves at least a minimal amount of interpretation.

This also means that Bible versions will vary somewhat on matters of punctuation. For the most part, however, there are enough grammatical clues in Hebrew and Greek sentences to determine with a high degree of certainty where these sentences begin and end. The larger decision translators face is the one discussed above, namely, whether to retain the longer sentences found in Greek or to break these into shorter ones for better English.

All versions, even the most literal ones, sometimes break up Greek sentences. For example, it is difficult to imagine how anyone could put Paul's impossibly long Greek sentence that makes up the entire thanksgiving in 2 Thessalonians 1:3–10 into one meaningful sentence in English. Even formal equivalent versions break it down in a variety of ways. The one translation that tried to keep the Greek sentence intact was the KJV, but to do so the translators used a variety of ploys (commas, semicolons, and colons) to clue the English reader into how the sentence works. In this they were followed by the American Standard Version (ASV, 1901). But most other English versions turn the single Greek sentence into several English ones, whether two (NKJV), four (RSV, NRSV, NASB, ESV), or more (REB: five; NLT, NET: six; NIV, TNIV: eight; GNT: nine).

The more difficult issue in this regard has to do with longer sense units (paragraphs and "chapters"). The "chapters" found in our Bibles were apparently first introduced into the Latin Vulgate by Stephen Langton (d. 1228), who did so for the obvious need to "find things" for the sake of citation. The verse numbers did not appear until some three centuries later, when they were introduced by Robert Stephens in his Greek-Latin New Testament of 1551. The first whole Bible to have verse numbers was Beza's Latin Bible of 1555; and the first to appear in English this way was the Geneva Bible (NT 1557; whole Bible 1560).

The unfortunate thing about this numbering system of chapters and verses was that it bypassed the more standard unit of thought beyond the sentence, namely, the paragraph. This shortcoming is particularly evident in the King James Version (followed by the NASB and NKJV), whose translators adopted the then recent (half-century old) practice of "canonizing" every numbered unit (a "verse") by setting it off as a paragraph. The result is an artificial division of the text into "verses" instead of a natural division into sentences and paragraphs.

Of course since paragraphs are not marked in the early Greek manuscripts, their identification is up to the discretion of translators. In an earlier time British and American authors in general, and nineteenth-century novelists in particular (e.g., Scott, Brontë, Hawthorne), tended toward very long paragraphs. In more recent times, the motto has become "shorter is better."

The tendency toward longer paragraphs found its expression in the American Standard Version (1901). These were slightly modified toward shorter paragraphs in its next revision, the Revised Standard Version (1946, 1952). Surprisingly, the paragraphing of the RSV tended to be kept intact by its two later, unrelated revisions (the NRSV and ESV). More recent translations not related to this tradition have tended toward shorter paragraphs (NIV, TNIV, NLT, NCV, etc.).

We should point out at the end of this section that the presence of chapter and verse numbers in our Bibles is a mixed blessing at best. They are, of course, absolutely essential for "finding things" and for everyone getting on the same page, as it were. But they have had an unfortunate history of promoting poor *reading* of the Bible by breaking the text down into artificial units. Our own instincts are that if these numbers were not present, Christians would read their Bibles far better than they now do.

A positive step in this direction is the common practice today of placing verse references unobtrusively in small, superscript type within natural paragraph divisions. An even better solution might be to place both chapter and verse divisions in the side margins, completely separate from the text itself. This would allow readers to find specific references, but would also encourage them to read biblical narratives as stories, New Testament epistles as real letters, and Hebrew psalms as poetry. This is how Scripture was intended to be read.

Translation or Transliteration

Another challenge facing Bible translators is how to handle certain Hebrew and Greek technical terms that are difficult to put into adequate English. At issue is whether to use (supposed) English equivalents or simply to transliterate them (i.e., to change the Hebrew or Greek letters into corresponding English ones). We have discussed the issue of transliteration with reference to weights, measures, and money in chapter 6. Here we consider several other technical terms.

Two such words occur together at the end of 1 Corinthians, which the KJV chose not to translate but to transliterate. They appear side by side, with an initial capital letter and without punctuation: "Let him be Anathema Maranatha" (1 Cor. 16:22). One wonders how the average reader could ever have understood that without help.

Anathema

The Greek term *anathema*, which occurs six times in the New Testament (Acts 23:14; Rom. 9:3; 1 Cor. 12:3; 16:22; Gal. 1:8, 9), is drawn from the Greek Old Testament, where it was used to translate Hebrew *cherem*. The Hebrew term could mean, positively, something "devoted to God," or negatively, something placed under God's ban and so destined for destruction (e.g., Judg. 6:18–7:15). In its six New Testament occurrences, *anathema* always carries this negative sense. Apart from the ASV, which transliterated the term as "anathema," most English versions consistently render it with some form of "curse/cursed/accursed" (NIV, TNIV, NET, ESV, NASU, REB, NJB, NAB, GW, GNT, NLT, etc.).

An exception appears in Galatians 1:8–9, where Paul calls down judgment against false teachers who are preaching a counterfeit gospel to the Galatians. While most versions keep the language of "cursed" (TNIV: "let that person be under God's curse" cf. NJB, NAB, ESV, NASU, NKJV, NLT), other versions translate it as the final outcome of the "curse": "let him be eternally condemned" (NIV); "let him be condemned to hell" (NET, GNT, GW, TEV). These latter two translations probably go too far, losing the connection to Paul's other uses of the term and moving beyond his intended meaning.

Maranatha (Marana Tha)

While only the KJV and ASV transliterate the word *anathema* in 1 Corinthians 16:22, several versions transliterate the word immediately after it: "Maranatha" (KJV, ASV, NASU, NAB, HCSB). This Greek word itself is a transliteration of an Aramaic phrase meaning, "Our Lord, come!" (*marana tha*) or "Our Lord has come" (*maran atha*). The surprising use by Paul of an Aramaic phrase in a letter written in Greek to Greek-speaking believers suggests to many scholars that the phrase is a traditional one that goes back to the early Aramaic-speaking church. If this is so, it would mean that the earliest church prayed to Jesus as their exalted "Lord" and expected his soon return. Transliterating the Aramaic phrase in these English versions apparently attempts to alert readers to this background. Most other versions simply translate the phrase as "Come, O Lord!" (NIV; cf. NKJV) or "Our Lord, come!" (NLT, NET, ESV, GW), sometimes with a footnote identifying the Aramaic words.

Sheol, Hades, Gehenna

These three words variously describe the place of the afterlife. *Sheol* is a Hebrew word that refers to "the place of the dead." The Septuagint translators rather consistently, and correctly, rendered it as *Hades* in Greek. *Gehenna*, by contrast, originally meant "the valley of Hinnom," a valley just south of Jerusalem where children were offered sacrificially to the "god" Molech during the Old Testament period (e.g., 2 Kings 23:10). By the time of Jesus this valley had become the city dump, where all kinds of garbage and things considered "unclean" (e.g., bodies of criminals) were burned.

As with many contemporary city dumps, the valley of Hinnom was a place of constant burning. Hence "Gehenna" became a word of abomination. When the idea of a future place of torment for the unbeliever took hold in the intertestamental period, this word was picked up to describe such a place, and it was so used by Jesus in the Gospels. Most modern versions have consistently rendered *gehenna* as "hell," with only the NAB transliterating it as "Gehenna" (cf. Matt. 5:22, 29, 30).

The treatment of the Hebrew term *Sheol* is more varied. The KJV translated the term thirty-one times in the Old Testament as "hell" (e.g., Deut. 32:22). This is not accurate since the word refers more generally to the place of the dead. A number of versions follow the ASV in simply transliterating it as "Sheol" (RSV, NRSV, NASB, NASU, ESV, NET, HCSB, NJB). One problem with this is that most English readers will have to consult a dictionary to find out what "Sheol" means. Other versions use a variety of expressions, depending on the context. In Psalm 16:10 we find "the grave" (NIV, NLT, CEV), "the power of death" (TEV), and "the realm of the dead" (TNIV). In Job 11:8 the term is translated variously as "the nether world" (NAB), "the underworld" (NLT), "the grave" (NIV, CEV), and "the world of the dead" (GNT).

The Divine Name

One of the great difficulties for Bible translators concerns how to render the divine name "Yahweh" into English. The God of the Old Testament, who first revealed himself to Moses at the burning bush (Ex. 3), at the same time revealed his Name—in the form of four Hebrew consonants *YHWH* (known as the *Tetragrammaton*, meaning "four letters"). Although the exact pronunciation is unknown, most scholars consider it to be "Yahweh."

For most of the period of the Old Testament, Israel regularly called on their God by this name. But for reasons not fully known to us (perhaps as a way of never disobeying the third commandment—against misusing God's name [Ex. 20:7]), after the exile the Jews became reluctant to use the name at all. Their way around it was orally to substitute the word *ʾadonai* ("Lord") whenever the divine name appeared in the biblical text. This had become the standard practice by the time the Hebrew Bible was translated into Greek for the Jewish communities of the Diaspora. Thus the translators rendered it with the Greek word *kyrios* ("Lord") and rather consistently did so without the article "the." The result was a Greek Bible where *kyrios*, not *ho kyrios* ("*the* Lord") was the way the divine name was known among all Greek-speaking Jews, including the writers of the New Testament.

But equally important for the early Christians was the fact that their primary confession was the short affirmation, "Jesus is Lord" (see Rom. 10:9; 1 Cor. 12:3; Phil. 2:10). That this came to have double meaning is evident in Paul's letters. Somewhere early on, Deuteronomy 6:4 had become the basic "theological confession" of Judaism: "Listen, Israel, Yahweh our God [*ʾelohim*], Yahweh is one." Well before the first Christian century, this confession had taken the form, "Listen, Israel, the LORD [*Yahweh* = *ʾadonai* = *kyrios*] your God, the LORD is One." In 1 Corinthians 8:6 Paul divides this confession into two parts, where "God" refers to the Father and "Lord" refers to the Son. In his letters, which are among the earliest documents in the New Testament, "Lord" (*kyrios*) almost always refers to Christ. The implication for Christology is that Paul uses the Old Testament name for God to describe Jesus Christ.

But this bit of history also created problems for the translators of the Bible into English, especially because the first attempts to do so (Wycliffe, Tyndale) were still based on the Latin Bible, where Yahweh had been consistently translated *Dominus* ("Lord"). This created a long tradition of using "Lord" to translate the Tetragrammaton in the Old Testament. The result was that God's name "Yahweh" is seldom found in the long history of English translation. The two exceptions are the ASV, which consistently rendered it "Jehovah," and the NJB, which chose to go with "Yahweh." ("Jehovah" is clearly a mispronunciation, resulting from the combination of the Hebrew vowel marks for *ʾadonai* with the Hebrew consonants *YHWH*.)

Most recent versions have maintained the historic practice that began with the KJV, to translate the divine name in the Old Testament as "the LORD" (small caps). So when readers see the word "Lord" in the Old

Testament, the Hebrew word behind it is (usually) *'adonai*; when they see "LORD," the Hebrew term is *YHWH*. Unfortunately, this practice has not generally been carried over to the citations of the Old Testament in the New. Since the New Testament writers followed the Septuagint in using Greek *kyrios* for both *'adonai* and *YHWH*, most English versions have followed suit, using "Lord" (lower case).

One exception is citations of Psalm 110:1, where a few versions distinguish between *YHWH* and *'adonai* by translating "LORD" and "Lord," respectively (KJV, NKJV, NLT; NLT does this elsewhere as well). The practice of not identifying *YHWH* in Old Testament quotations in the New has some unfortunate Christological consequences, since in most cases in Paul's letters the reference is to the risen Lord, Jesus Christ. The implications of Christ's deity intended by Paul might be missed by the modern reader.

Capitalization

The tradition of capitalizing certain words in English has had a long and varied history. In earlier centuries far more nouns were capitalized than is currently true, and the number keeps decreasing.

Although the KJV did not capitalize pronouns used for God, several contemporary versions have adopted this practice (NASB, NASU, NKJV, HCSB). (Other versions in the KJV tradition do not: RSV, NRSV, ESV.) Most English stylists advise that all pronouns—including those for deity—should be kept in lowercase.

Capitalizing pronouns with reference to Jesus in the New Testament can also create problems. Although the goal of emphasizing Christ's deity in this way is a noble one in theory, in practice it can distort the meaning of the text. For example, when the scribes and the Pharisees say to Jesus, "We want to see a sign from You" (Matt. 12:38 NASU), the capitalized "You" implies that the *Pharisees* think Jesus is divine. But, of course, they do not. Whenever an individual in the Gospels speaks about Jesus, or to him, capitalized pronouns can misrepresent the meaning of the text.

Difficulties also arise when capitalizing pronouns in messianic prophecies in the Old Testament. For example, Psalm 22:1 in the NKJV reads, "My God, My God, why have You forsaken Me?" The first problem is that there is inconsistency here, since pronouns in other passages (see Pss. 16:10; 41:9) are not capitalized in the NKJV, even though they are identified as messianic prophecies in the New Testament (Acts 2:27; John 13:18).

The second problem, however, is that many of these prophecies are fulfilled "typologically," rather than uniquely, in Christ. In other words, the original referent in the Old Testament might be David or righteous sufferers in general. Jesus is indeed the "fulfillment" of these prophecies in that he is the last and greatest in the line of Davidic kings, and the last and greatest of righteous sufferers. But capitalizing pronouns might wrongly suggest that the original human referents (like David) are themselves divine. It seems best therefore to follow the now standard practice of leaving all pronouns in lowercase letters.

Exegetical Uncertainties and the Use of Footnotes

In chapter 8 we pointed out the difficulties that scholars sometimes have in choosing between variant readings in the manuscript tradition. There we also noted that the alternative reading could often be found in a footnote in the more recent versions. The phenomenon of offering translational alternatives, or other information, in footnotes goes back to the KJV, ASV, etc. The ASV uses them for the following reasons:

1. To offer alternative readings where the textual tradition differs, or in the case of the Old Testament where there is a significantly different reading in one of the versions.
2. To offer alternative translations for the same text, when the committee was divided.
3. To offer verse location when a New Testament writer cites the Old Testament.
4. To offer explanations of difficult words or phrases, especially when the biblical idea is no longer a common one.
5. To explain the meaning of some biblical names.
6. To offer references "to other passages, which are either strictly parallel, or serve the purpose of illustrating or justifying a particular rendering."
7. To offer a more literal rendition of a Greek or Hebrew word or phrase, where, apparently, the translators thought something was lost in translation.

Most of these, although rarely no. 5, are found in some form or another in contemporary versions, although each will have its own concerns and emphases. Some translations are especially spare with reference to notes (REB, NAB, NASU), while others (e.g., NRSV, TNIV) have moved in the other direction, offering a broader range of help for the modern reader. The NET Bible, with almost 61,000 footnotes of various kinds, certainly has the most expansive notes among contemporary versions. Readers would do well to consult the preface of whatever version they are reading to determine the reasons notes were included and the manner in which these are presented.

The five most common reasons for footnotes in contemporary versions are to provide: (1) textual variants, (2) references for Old Testament citations, (3) alternative interpretations, (4) explanatory comments, and (5) formal equivalent alternatives for idiomatic translations. All five of these can be illustrated from Mark 1 in the TNIV:

1. A note on Mark 1:1 in the TNIV indicates that "many manuscripts" add the phrase "*Son of God*" to the introductory phrase. Most other versions also provide notes alerting the reader to this important textual question.
2. A note at the end of Mark 1:3 provides a reference for an Old Testament citation, informing the reader that the quotation beginning with "a voice of one calling in the wilderness" comes from Isaiah 40:3.
3. A footnote to the word "tempted" in the description of Jesus' temptation in the desert by Satan (Mark 1:13) offers the alternate interpretation that "The Greek for *tempted* can also mean *tested*."
4. An explanatory comment appears in a footnote on the word "leprosy" in Mark 1:40, where the reader is informed, "The Greek word traditionally translated *leprosy* was used for various diseases affecting the skin."
5. A note on the word "evil" in the phrase "evil spirit" (1:23) provides a more formal equivalent rendering, "Greek *unclean*." As discussed in chapter 6, an "unclean spirit" is an evil and defiling demon in opposition to God.

A sixth, much less common, reason for adding a note is to inform the reader that the meaning of a particular word or phrase is uncertain (usually a rare Hebrew word). For example, a note in the TNIV on the word "body" in Job 21:24 ("well nourished in body") reads: "The meaning of the Hebrew for this word is uncertain." The reason for this note becomes clear when one considers the variety of ways contemporary versions translate the word (in italics):

"his *loins* full of milk" (NRSV)
"His *figure* is full and nourished" (NAB)
"his *pails* full of milk" (ESV)
"*thighs* padded with fat" (NJB)
"his *sides* are filled out with fat" (NASU)
"his *body* is well fed" (HCSB)

These examples should be enough to cause the reader to consult the preface of his or her translation so as to understand the purpose and nature of footnotes in the translation.

"Red Letter" Editions

The final item of format in this chapter generally lies outside the control of translators—who are concerned with the words, sentences, and paragraphs—and in the hands of publishers. This is the matter of "red letter" editions of Scripture. In terms of the production of Scripture, red letter editions are a recent phenomenon, whose beginnings date from the turn of the twentieth century.

The idea itself began with the longtime editor and publisher of the *Christian Herald* magazine, Louis Klopsch, who in 1899 first published a King James Version in which all the words of Christ were printed in red. This was the result of an unusual kind of piety, where the red was intended to remind people of Jesus' blood that had been poured out for them. But the result was to create several strange ironies in North American Christianity.

First, here were people who believed strongly in the full divine inspiration of *all* of Scripture, yet they were willing to set out the words of Jesus in such a way that they seemed to have pride of place over the rest of Scripture. So while the whole Bible is Spirit-inspired, the "actual words" of Jesus seem to have a place of significance above those of the biblical writers themselves. For most biblical scholars that borders on a false understanding of the doctrine of inspiration.

Second, the words that appear in red in these editions are rarely the actual words of Jesus. Rather, his own words, spoken in a Galilean dialect of Aramaic, had already been *translated* into Greek for the Greek-speaking communities for whom the Gospels were intended. The few Aramaic words of Jesus that are preserved (mostly in Mark) are transliterated Aramaic (5:41, *Talitha koum*; 7:34, *Ephphatha*; 14:35, *Abba*; 15:34, *Eloi, Eloi, lema sabachthani*), followed by a translation into Greek. So, for example, Mark 14:36 has Jesus' words in an Aramaic transliteration (*abba*), which Mark then translates into Greek (*pater*), but which we must now put into English ("Father").

So in terms of biblical inspiration, what Jesus said is an extremely important part of the Story, but not more important than the Story itself in which the words are encased. One also wonders why God the Father has been left out here. Should not his words in the Old Testament and the New be printed in a distinct color?

It is hardly surprising, therefore, that most translators are opposed to red-letter editions because of the mixed theological, not to mention devotional, signals they send. But publishers continue to issue them because "this is what the people want," despite the protests of translators. Perhaps this discussion will be of some help on this matter.

The following two chapters, which briefly outline the story of English translations, recount both the history of putting the Bible into English and descriptions of what we consider to be the primary efforts to do so in the past half century.

For Further Reading

Barker, Kenneth, and Edwin Palmer, eds. *The NIV: The Making of a Contemporary Translation*. Grand Rapids: Zondervan, 1986.

Part 5

The Bible in English

Chapter 10

A Brief History of the Bible in English

Although the story of the Bible in English has been told many times and in many places, the nature of this book requires that it be told once more. However, rather than write out that history in detail, we have chosen to summarize it with two concerns in mind: (1) to overview the data so the reader will appreciate the rich history of English Bible translation, and (2) to point out how often this endeavor has been embroiled in controversy. We do this not because we love controversy, but to remind the reader of how important is Scripture in one's native tongue, and therefore how often a "revision" has been met with resistance. While this resistance is the result of people's love for their Bibles—meaning the ones they have always used and are used to—it has much too often been accompanied with anger and animosity.

Much of the present overview will be in summary form, but because of their importance, the earliest versions receive a bit more attention. This chapter's overview carries through to the appearance of the Revised Standard Version in 1948 (NT) and 1952 (whole Bible). In the next chapter we will overview some of the translations that have appeared in the last fifty years.

The English Bible before Printing

The first two Bibles to appear in English are both associated with the name of John Wycliffe. A very "wooden," literal version appeared just before his death in 1384. A more idiomatic, and therefore more readable, version appeared shortly afterward—basically the work of Wycliffe's secretary, John Purvey. Given the times (pre-Reformation) and circumstances (pre-printing press), this latter Bible had a relatively wide circulation, when one considers that every copy had to be created by hand. It was also a translation from the Latin Bible, since the Greek Bible was used exclusively by the Eastern Church and did not make its way to the West until after the fall of Constantinople to the Turks in 1453.

It is of interest to note here that the tension between translations into English that are either "literal" or "meaning-based" goes back to the very beginning. Wycliffe himself was responsible for, and obviously preferred, the more "literal" version. This was due in part to his political philosophy that the Bible was basically the codification of God's law and should thus have a "legal" ring to it. Yet it was the latter version, the more idiomatic one, that won the day, since most people found it more useful.

The First Printed Bibles

The first printed Bible was in fact one of the first books printed by Johannes Gutenberg, the inventor of the printing press; it appeared in 1456. This was the Latin Bible, which was the only Bible used by the Church of Rome. But once the Reformation with its emphasis on Scripture took hold in northern Europe, vernacular translations began to appear, beginning with Luther's German New Testament, published in 1522 (the complete Bible in 1534).

The work of putting the Bible into English, based on the original languages, was taken up by William Tyndale — but not in England, since Henry VIII remained within the Roman Catholic Church until 1534. Tyndale, in exile in Belgium, was arrested there and in 1536 was executed as a heretic. His martyrdom reminds us that many have paid the ultimate price to make God's Word available to everyone.

Despite the death of its translator, Tyndale's version was so carefully and well done that it rapidly assumed a life of its own. Eventually, his translation served as the basis for almost all subsequent English versions up to the twentieth century, including the King James Version of 1611, which is estimated to be about ninety percent Tyndale. In the twentieth and twenty-first centuries that tradition continued through the American Standard Version and its successors (RSV, NASB, NASU, NRSV, ESV). In fact, before the KJV there had been earlier attempts among Protestants to offer a standardized version of Scripture in English, and all but one of these (the Geneva Bible) were based on Tyndale's version. These can be surveyed by date and name, with a brief historical note about each.

The Coverdale Bible (1535; 2nd ed. 1537). Coverdale, a friend and helper of Tyndale and an English clergyman, made Tyndale's version available in England, but not under Tyndale's name. Coverdale used Tyndale for the Pentateuch and the New Testament; the rest of the Bible was translated from Latin and German versions, since Coverdale himself had no expertise in Greek and Hebrew. The second edition was published "with the king's most gracious licence."

Matthew's Bible (approx. 1537). This was Tyndale's completed version, published in England by another of Tyndale's colleagues, John Rogers, but under the pseudonym "Thomas Matthew." After all, it would have been impolitic for "Tyndale" to arrive in England under the name of one of his coworkers.

The Great Bible (1539; 7th ed. 1541). This Bible was also the work of Coverdale, but now sponsored by the Church of England as its official version. It was called "The Great Bible" because of its unusually large size (to sit on church lecterns). It was a slight revision of "Matthew's Bible." Tyndale's work, once banned, was now the basis for the official Bible of the Church of England!

The Geneva Bible (1560). This important version was primarily the work of William Whittingham, one of the exiles of Mary Tudor's reign (1553–58). It was the first version in which all of the Old Testament was translated directly from the Hebrew text and was such a superior work to those preceding it that it had a considerable history of its own. It became the official Bible of the Church of Scotland (Presbyterian), was the only Bible of the dissenters, and thus was brought to New England by the Pilgrims (and is rightly to be found on the tables of the restored Plymouth colony). It was also the Bible of Shakespeare, and its language and cadences can be found throughout his plays and sonnets. In many circles it continued to be the Bible of use for a generation or more after the KJV became the "official" English version.

The Bishops' Bible (1568). This version, the official Anglican response to the Geneva Bible, was initiated by Matthew Parker, Archbishop of Canterbury. It was the first version where the various sections were delegated to Hebrew and Greek experts to be translated. All of these translators were, or were to become, Anglican bishops. The revisers were to use translations already in use, including the Geneva Bible, but were to eliminate the (sometimes antagonistic) footnotes of the latter. Although the Bishop's Bible went through nineteen editions and superseded the Great Bible as the official Bible of the Church, it was seldom used outside the Anglican communion because of the superior quality of the Geneva Bible.

The Douai-Rheims Version (1582; OT 1609). This version was produced by Gregory Martin, one of several Roman Catholic scholars who sought refuge in Northern France during the Elizabethan era. For all practical purposes it became the "KJV" of the English-speaking Roman Catholic Church through the mid-twentieth century. Although it was a translation of the Latin Vulgate rather than the Greek and Hebrew, it shows remarkable similarity to the Bishop's Bible and to the King James

Version, as one can see by reading it side-by-side with the KJV (cf. *The Precise Parallel New Testament*, ed. John R. Kohlenberger III [New York: Oxford Univ. Press, 1995]).

The King James Version (1611)

By far the most important translation of the Bible into English was the King James Version, which first appeared in 1611 as the "Authorized Version." Although it was about ninety percent "Tyndale," it was in fact a careful revision, ultimately based on the original languages and done by the ablest biblical scholars of the Anglican Church. Especially important, it was also "authorized" from the outset (1603) by King James I himself. At least one of the reasons it tended to find more universal acceptance is that the translators (wisely) chose not to include the kinds of controversial theological marginal notes that could be found in most of its predecessors.

As with most of these versions, however, in some quarters the KJV met strong resistance. Yet in time it took its place as perhaps the most significant work ever published in English. So well done was it that it not only held pride-of-place in almost all English-speaking churches for centuries, but it also helped to shape the English language for the next four centuries. Consider a few of the many idioms that have entered the English language through the KJV:

fall flat on your face (Num. 22:31)
escape by the skin of my teeth (Job 19:20)
a fly in the ointment (Eccl. 10:1)
pride goes before a fall (Prov. 16:18)
sour grapes (Ezek. 18:2)
pour out your heart (Ps. 62:8)
everything under the sun (Eccl. 1:3, 9, 14, etc.)

Those who resisted the KJV were people from more conservative expressions of Christian faith, who were not ready to accept anything that came out of the official Church of England and under the auspices of the king. It is therefore of some historical interest that in the twentieth century in the United States, it was similar groups who resisted contemporary translations that deviated from the "real Bible," the King James Version!

It should also finally be noted that all of these versions of the New Testament that were made directly from the Greek text were based on what came to be known as the *Textus Receptus* or the "Received Text." What they have in common is the translation of a late Greek text that had accumulated centuries of variations from the original text (see chap. 8 above). These textual variations represent the main difference between the KJV and the modern versions that began to appear with the Revised Version of 1881. For many this textual issue was the primary point of contention between the KJV and its subsequent revisions.

From the Revised Version to the Revised Standard Version

The history of English versions between 1881 and 1952 has two, quite unrelated, parts to it. First, there is the continuing tradition of "revising" existing Bibles, which began with the *Coverdale Bible* and carried through the King James Version and its successors: the Revised Version (RV, 1885), the American Standard Version (ASV, 1901), the Revised Standard Version (RSV, 1952), the New American Standard Bible (NASB, 1971), the New King James Version (NKJV, 1982), the New Revised Standard Version (NRSV, 1989), and the English Standard Version (ESV, 2001). In this way the long tradition of translations based on "formal equivalence" was maintained throughout the twentieth century right into the beginning of the twenty-first.

Second, beginning with the remarkable *Twentieth Century New Testament* (1901), a new movement in Bible translation began, where the goal was simultaneously to be faithful to the meaning of the original text but also to render it in contemporary English. Following this version, a remarkable number of new versions began to appear, either of the whole Bible or parts of it. In *So Many Versions?* written by Sakae Kubo and Walter F. Specht (Grand Rapids: Zondervan, 1983), a guide to the better-known twentieth-century versions, an appendix includes no less than seventy-six such versions that appeared in English between 1901 and the Revised Standard Version in 1952.

We will note here only a few of the more significant versions within these two streams of tradition ("significant" in the sense that they had a degree of broader use in Great Britain and/or the United States).

The Revised Version (RV) (1881/1885). The first major revision of the KJV took place in England toward the end of the nineteenth century. It had been initiated by the Anglican Convocation of Canterbury in 1870. Its aim was to produce an updated KJV, where the Old Testament continued to be based on the standard Hebrew text (the Masoretic text) while the New Testament was based on an updated Greek text produced by B. F. Westcott and F. J. A. Hort, both of whom were on the revision committee. Their Greek text was actually published five days before the revised New Testament appeared in 1881.

This revision, which in time was to become the standard Bible in Great Britain, ended up as something of a mixed blessing. Because of many advances in Hebrew scholarship over the preceding two centuries, the Old Testament was a considerable improvement over the KJV, making clear many places that were obscure in the KJV. But the New Testament turned out to be only a partial improvement. On the one hand, because of the textual expertise of Westcott and Hort, the New Testament now had a much more reliable Greek text than the Textus Receptus (the Greek text behind the KJV). On the other hand, eagerness for grammatical precision sometimes superseded the need to be clear in English. Thus the end result was a translation based on a superior Greek text, but one that many people considered to be quite inferior to the KJV in terms of English literary quality.

But perhaps the greatest failing of all was the determination of the revisers to make this a *revision* of the King James Version rather than a genuinely new translation. In so doing they adopted what has been dubbed as "an archaizing policy," in which they would use no "modern" expression in English that was not current in 1611. Not only did this inhibit genuine revision, but it kept the Bible from being updated to the language of the day. The result was that even though the Revised Version was initially received with great enthusiasm, it turned out to be more of a scholar's Bible than one used by everyday readers. Most people found the familiarity of the KJV much more to their liking. Indeed, Charles Spurgeon is reported to have said that the Revised Version "was strong in Greek but weak in English."

The American Standard Version (ASV) (1901). Early on the British revisers of the Revised Version reached out to their American counterparts to join in the revision process, and an American committee was formed. But because the Atlantic had to be crossed by steamship rather than aircraft, the two committees never met together. Instead, the British draft was sent to the American committee, who then returned it with the committee's suggestions. Since this became an unworkable scheme, American input into the Revised Version was minimal. The American committee chose to produce its own version of the Revised Version, but because of an agreement with their British counterparts, they had to wait fourteen years to publish it.

Work on the American version began in 1897 and was published in 1901 as the American Standard Version. The hope was that it would eventually replace the KJV on the American side of the Atlantic. And while this translation chose not to be bound by the archaizing policy of the Revised Version, it was still a *revision*, not a new translation. The revisers chose to keep hundreds of KJV renderings that had fallen out of English usage by the end of the nineteenth century. For example, they kept such archaisms as "he hungered" in Matthew 21:18. The ASV's greatest idiosyncrasy was rendering the Divine Name in the Old Testament as "Jehovah" instead of as "LORD." Since this vocalizing of the Divine Name soon fell out of favor with biblical scholars, the ASV introduced a name for God that was seldom used by anyone except the cult known as Jehovah's Witnesses.

The Twentieth Century New Testament (1900/1904). Above we described this version as "remarkable," which indeed it was. Aptly named for the new century in which it appeared, its remarkable nature was that what turned out to be an impressive rendering of the New Testament into contemporary English had no professional biblical scholars on the committee. It was primarily the work of laypeople, who were in time joined by a few ministers and whose work was eventually reviewed by two biblical scholars and the classicist R. F. Weymouth. The concern of the two well-educated people primarily responsible for producing this version was for their own children, who found the Revised Version out of reach in terms of understanding. Thus was born a version that sought to do in English what Luther had attempted in German nearly four centuries earlier (see pp. 30, 136 above)—to produce a truly idiomatic version.

Another thing that made this work remarkable was that it was the work of a "committee" that never met together as one. Rather, the NT documents had been portioned out to individual translators, whose work was then passed through the committee for corrections and improvements. Work that began in the mid-1890s was eventually published in three parts between 1898 and 1900. After receiving a great many suggestions from readers, a revised New Testament appeared in 1904. Among other innovations the translators presented the text in paragraphs, with numbers in the margins, and rearranged the books within traditional groupings in what was assumed to be their chronological order. While this version enjoyed a good measure of success in Great Britain, it was scarcely noticed in North America, until an "Americanized" version was published by Moody Press in 1961, where the traditional order of the books was restored. It is still a translation worth reading, or at least consulting.

The New Testament in Modern Speech (R. F. Weymouth; 1903). This excellent translation was the first of many to follow that were the work of a single scholar. Weymouth had been headmaster of a "nonconformist" British private school, who was equally concerned about his students' ability to understand the English Bible in its traditional wordings, either the KJV or RV. A classicist by training, he set out to provide his students with a New Testament they could understand. The result was *The New Testament in Modern Speech: An Idiomatic Translation into Every-day English.* Although Weymouth died in 1902 before the finished product was printed, a close friend, and member of the Twentieth Century New Testament committee, made the final revisions and saw the work through to publication. Like the Twentieth Century New Testament, it is still worth reading today.

The New Testament: A New Translation (James Moffatt; 1913/1926 [rev. ed. 1935]). This second significant New Testament to be translated by a single individual was at once both a work of the highest order and one full of idiosyncrasies. Among other things, it was based on the Greek text of H. von Soden, itself an idiosyncratic text. Moffatt was also quite ready to accept emendations of various kinds to the text, including the rearranging of some verses and the omission of others. It also had several very Scottish renderings (e.g., barrister, cairn, hie, kilt). Although idiosyncratic, Moffatt's version was also engaging and stimulating. It achieved considerable popular success, including a commentary series based on its text.

The New Testament: An American Translation (E. J. Goodspeed; 1923/1927). This version, like Moffatt's, was produced by a brilliant New Testament scholar. As the title indicates, it was as intentionally American as Moffatt's was Scottish. Despite the occasional idiosyncrasy that occurs in any single-person translation of the Bible, this version rightfully took its place among the better ones and enjoyed many printings. Although it was the work of a noted scholar, the English was readily accessible to the average American and enabled many American readers to read the Bible afresh, as if for the first time.

The Centenary Translation of the New Testament (Helen Barrett Montgomery; 1924). This fourth translation of the New Testament by a single individual is seldom noted in the literature, in part because its appearance coincided with the centenary celebration of the American Baptists, and thus it was perceived to be more "denominational." But it is worth noting here if for no other reason than the fact that it was the first translation of the New Testament by a woman scholar. Among the many helps she offered the reader was italicizing of citations of the Old Testament by New Testament authors. She is perhaps best known for considering 1 Corinthians 14:34–35 as Paul's quoting from the Corinthians' letter to him. Overall this is an excellent translation, altogether less idiosyncratic than Moffatt, and still worth reading or consulting.

The Holy Bible: A Translation from the Latin Vulgate (Ronald A. Knox; 1945/1949). The last of the pre-RSV versions to be noted here is this significant Roman Catholic translation by a British monsignor of well-known literary skills. His translation was based on the Latin Vulgate, since Knox was already well on his way to finishing the New Testament portion of the translation when a papal decree in 1943 opened the way for Roman Catholics to translate from the original Hebrew and Greek. What he produced, in fact, was the first approved translation of the Bible into English since the Douai-Rheims version of 1582/1609. Sometimes quite paraphrastic, Knox's version was an excellent, literary translation that was also readily accessible to all.

The Revised Standard Version (NT 1948; full 1952). The present overview of English translations comes to its proper conclusion with the appearance of the whole Bible in this version. Although it was strongly opposed by some conservative American Christians, the RSV became the Bible of choice for much of American Christendom during the third quarter of the twentieth century.

Its strength, however, was also its primary drawback. As the name implies, it was intended to be in the long line of English Bible revisions traced back to William Tyndale. The translators were in fact "revisers," and although they were free to offer what scholarship believed to be the best sense of the text, they were also compelled to stay close to the KJV literary tradition as that had come to them through the RV and ASV. The result was actually better than one might have expected from such a hybrid. So it was no surprise that for the majority of American Christians who were not still wedded to the KJV, this became their preferred Bible, and for a few decades was the best-selling English version after the KJV.

By the time the latest revision appeared in 1972—a revision that succeeded in becoming a "common Bible" for both Protestants and Roman Catholics—the English language itself was also changing at a remarkably rapid pace. So the RSV, too, had to undergo a thorough revision within two decades. But that part of the story is for our next, and final, chapter.

For Further Reading

Bruce, F. F. *History of the Bible in English.* New York: Oxford University Press, 1978.

Metzger, Bruce M. *The Bible in Translation: Ancient and English Versions.* Grand Rapids: Baker, 2001.

Chapter 11

Contemporary Bible Versions

The publication of the Revised Standard Version in 1952 marks the beginning of a new era in Bible translation. No version up to this point had seriously challenged the dominance of the KJV. Although the RSV did not come close to usurping its predecessor, its use of better manuscripts and its greater accuracy at many points taught readers that a modern version could actually improve upon the venerable KJV tradition. In this way it set a precedent for revision and refinement that continues today.

Also important for translators in the second half of the twentieth century were advances in the fields of linguistics and cultural anthropology. Biblical scholars have benefited greatly from the insights of missiologists and international Bible translators concerning how language works and how best to translate from one language to another. Especially notable here is the work of groups like Wycliffe Bible Translators, the United Bible Societies, and other international translation organizations.

There are various ways to classify contemporary English Bible versions: by date, relationship to predecessors, denominational association, or translation philosophy. While the RSV, NASB, NKJV, NRSV, and ESV are revisions in the KJV tradition but consulting original biblical languages, other versions are freshly translated directly from the Hebrew or Greek. The following chart shows these relationships:

Contemporary English Versions Categorized by Relationship

(Date is first edition of whole Bible)

Revisions in the KJV Tradition	New Versions	Revisions of New Versions
Revised Standard Version: RSV (1952)	Jerusalem Bible: JB (1966)	New Jerusalem Bible: NJB (1986)
New American Standard Bible: NASB, NASU (1971/1995)	New English Bible: NEB (1970)	Revised English Bible: REB (1989)
New King James Version: NKJV (1982)	New American Bible: NAB (1970)	
New Revised Standard Version: NRSV (1990)	The Living Bible: LB (1971)	New Living Translation: NLT (1996)
English Standard Version: ESV (2001)	Good News Translation: GNT: (also TEV/ GNB; 1976)	
	New International Version: NIV (1978)	Today's NIV: TNIV (2005)
	New Century Version: NCV (1986)	
	God's Word: GW (1995)	
	Contemporary English Version: CEV (1995)	
	The Message (2002)	
	Holman Christian Standard Bible: HCSB (2004)	
	New English Translation: NET (2005)	

One benefit of a fresh translation from the Hebrew and Greek is the tendency to remove archaic or traditional language that does not clearly reproduce the meaning of the original text. One perceived weakness is that these versions do not always sound like the "real Bible," that is, the Bible readers are familiar with (i.e., the KJV tradition). Of course this detriment can also be an asset, since the Bible did not sound like Elizabethan English to its original readers.

In this chapter we will survey contemporary versions according to their translation theory, moving from formal equivalent, to mediating, to functional equivalent. The twenty-five versions discussed below do not represent an exhaustive list. We have included only those versions that are widely available. The dates beside each version indicate the publication for the full Bible. For convenient reference, we reproduce here the translation spectrum that appeared in chapter 2.

Formal Equivalent				Mediating				Functional Equivalent	
NASB	KJV	RSV	NAB	NIV	JB	NEB		GNT	LB
NASU	NKJV	ESV NRSV		TNIV	NJB	REB	NLT	CEV	
		Tanakh HCSB NET				GW	NCV	The Message	

Formal Equivalent Versions

New American Standard Bible (1971; rev. 1995). As noted in the previous chapter, the RSV was a revision of the ASV, but some conservatives perceived it as containing a liberal bias. So a group of conservative scholars decided to produce a second revision of the ASV. The result was the New American Standard Bible. The NASB was prepared by fifty-eight originally anonymous, but now acknowledged, scholars under the auspices of the Lockman Foundation of La Habra, California. The New Testament appeared in 1963 and the whole Bible in 1971.

The twofold purpose of the editorial board was "to adhere as closely as possible to the original languages of the Holy Scripture, and to make the translation in a fluent and readable style according to current English usage" (foreword to the NASB). By most assessments, the version succeeds in the first goal but fails in the second. The NASB is the most consistently literal or formal equivalent of major English versions produced over the last half century. Examples of this include its use of italicization of English words that do not have Greek or Hebrew parallels and the identification of historical present tense verbs in the New Testament with an asterisk. But it lacks clarity and readability.

An updated edition of the NASB, designated NASU, was released in 1995. It increased readability somewhat and removed some archaic language, including the "thees" and "thous" that had been retained with reference to God in the original NASB.

New King James Version (1982). While the NASB was a revision of the ASV (itself a revision of the KJV), a direct revision of the KJV was initiated by Arthur Farstad and sponsored by Thomas Nelson Publishers of Nashville, Tennessee. The NKJV was produced by more than 130 evangelical scholars working over a seven-year period. The New Testament appeared in 1979 and the whole Bible followed in 1982.

The primary distinction of the NKJV is its textual base; it used the Textus Receptus, the edition of the Greek New Testament behind the KJV. As discussed in chapter 8, other modern versions use the critical text derived from older Greek manuscripts. To its credit, footnotes in the NKJV alert the reader to different readings in the critical text. While updating archaic words, especially the "thees" and "thous," the NKJV consciously seeks to retain the cadence, style, and idiom of the KJV. The result is one of the most formal equivalent of modern versions.

New Revised Standard Version (1990). After the publication of the RSV in 1952, its translation committee continued to meet every few years to consider future changes and to make minor corrections to the text. In 1974 the National Council of Churches, copyright holder of the RSV, authorized a revision. New Testament scholar Bruce Metzger served as chairman of the translation committee. The complete Bible was published in 1990. Like its predecessors, the NRSV is a formal equivalent version. It was also the first English version to consistently and comprehensively introduce gender inclusive language for masculine generic terms in Hebrew and Greek. It is widely used in academic and scholarly circles.

English Standard Version (2001). Some conservatives were unhappy with the perceived liberalism of the RSV, but felt that the NASB was too literal. They also considered the trend toward gender inclusive language in the NRSV to be a detriment rather than an asset. So they sought permission from the National Council of Churches to revise the 1971 edition of the RSV. Permission was granted and the resulting translation was named the English Standard Version.

This revision moved the text of the RSV in a more conservative and evangelical direction. Approximately 7 percent of the RSV has been changed. In addition to "correcting" certain RSV readings—such as returning "virgin" to Isaiah 7:14 and "propitiation" to Romans 3:25—the ESV removes "thees" and "thous" with reference to deity and updates other archaic language. It also moves the text in a slightly more literal direction. The ESV adopts a moderate, though sometimes inconsistent, use of gender inclusive language. It is published by Crossway books, a division of Good News Publishers.

The Amplified Bible (1965). The Amplified Bible is unique among Bible versions in that it provides "amplifications"—synonyms and explanations in brackets and parentheses within the text. Based on the ASV, the Amplified Bible was largely the work of Mrs. Frances Siewert. It was published in stages between 1954 and 1965. A slightly updated edition was released in 1987.

The strength of this version is that it acknowledges that no single English word or phrase can capture precisely the meaning of the Hebrew or Greek. Its weakness is that it gives readers the false impression that Hebrew and Greek words are "packed" with theological content and can mean many things at once. Another weakness is that readers may simply pick whichever meaning they like instead of discerning the single correct meaning that fits the context. The New Testament of the Amplified Bible was sponsored by the Lockman Foundation, the same organization that later produced the NASB; the Old Testament was sponsored by Zondervan Publishers.

Mediating Versions

New International Version (1978; rev. 1984). The NIV was the result of a trans-denominational effort by approximately a hundred scholars, sponsored by the New York Bible Society (now the International Bible Society). Each book was translated by a separate team of experts, then submitted to three successive editorial committees. Since its editors represented many different denominations, the translation was relatively free from sectarian bias. A smaller Committee on Bible Translation (CBT) of approximately fifteen members continued to examine and update the text. The New Testament was released in 1973 and the whole Bible in 1978. A minor revision was released in 1984.

The NIV came to be widely used and by the mid-1980s began outselling the KJV. Twenty-five years after its release more than 110 million copies were in print. The NIV's popularity was due in part to its finding a niche between the formal and functional equivalent versions available at the time. The NIV was clear and readable, yet still close enough to the rhythm and cadence of the KJV to sound like "the real Bible" (that is, the KJV!).

Today's New International Version (2005). The Committee on Bible Translation intended to periodically update the NIV in order to keep up with changes in the English language and advances in biblical scholarship. These revisions, it was assumed, would include the gradual adoption of gender accurate language (see chapter 7). Controversy erupted in 1997, however, when a gender inclusive version of the NIV (*NIV Inclusive*

Language Edition, or NIVI) was introduced in Great Britain by publisher Hodder & Stoughton. Facing negative publicity generated by *World* magazine and strong opposition from certain conservative groups, the International Bible Society (the NIV copyright holder) and Zondervan decided to freeze the NIV in its 1984 edition and to release instead Today's New International Version (TNIV)—a new and revisable edition of the NIV.

The TNIV will now carry forward the revision policy of the NIV, periodically updating the text in light of changes in English, advances in biblical scholarship, and greater accuracy and clarity. The New Testament was released in 2001 and the whole Bible in 2005. The TNIV has changed about 7 percent of the NIV text, with approximately one third of these revisions related to gender. More significantly, hundreds of changes were made toward greater exegetical accuracy. Each of the biblical books was assigned to two evangelical scholars with expertise on that book. Their proposed revisions were then brought to the committee, where an 80 percent majority was needed to make any change.

The result is a translation that maintains the readability of the NIV but which has achieved a higher level of accuracy in meaning. For example, in 1 Corinthians 7:1 the Greek euphemism for sexual intercourse, "to touch a woman," has been changed from the questionable rendering "to marry" to a contemporary euphemism "to have sexual relations with a woman" and put in quotes, since it comes from the Corinthians' letter to Paul.

Holman Christian Standard Bible (2004). The HCSB was produced by the Sunday School Board of the Southern Baptist Convention (SBC) and was intended to serve as an alternative to the NIV for Southern Baptist curriculum and ministry. It is published by Broadman & Holman, the publishing wing of the SBC. The HCSB is generally more literal than the NIV or NET but less so than the formal equivalent versions surveyed above. According to its introduction, the HCSB strives for neither formal nor functional equivalence, but "optimal equivalence":

> Optimal equivalence starts with an exhaustive analysis of the text at every level (word, phrase, clause, sentence, discourse) in the original language to determine its original meaning and intention (or purpose). Then relying on the latest and best language tools and experts, the nearest corresponding semantic and linguistic equivalents are used to convey as much of the information and intention of the original text with as much clarity and readability as possible. This process assures the maximum transfer of both the words and thoughts contained in the original.

This commendable description sounds a great deal like the goal of functional equivalence: striving to reproduce the *meaning* of the text as accurately and clearly as possible.

Though following the critical Greek text, the HCSB is unique among modern versions in supplying many alternative readings from the Textus Receptus and the Majority Text in its footnotes (cf. NKJV).

New English Translation or *NET Bible* (2005). The NET Bible is an online Bible translation sponsored by the Biblical Studies Foundation (Bible.org) and produced by more than twenty biblical scholars. The NET's most distinctive feature is its inclusion of almost 61,000 notes, which provide interpretive options, alternative renderings, and other insights into the Hebrew and Greek texts. The rationale is that since something is always lost in translation, these notes allow the reader to "look over the translator's shoulder" at the process of translation.

In addition to translation notes, the NET also provides study notes, text-critical notes, and map notes. The acronym "NET" is a play on words, referring both to the version's name — *New English Translation* — and to its Internet format. Although primarily an Internet version, the NET Bible is also available in print. The version went through two preliminary "Beta" editions before an official "First Edition" was released in November 2005.

New English Bible (1970). Two British versions, the NEB and its revision the REB, also occupy a place near the center of the translation spectrum. In May 1946, the same year the New Testament of the RSV was published, a motion was presented to the General Assembly of the Church of Scotland to produce a new version of the Bible in contemporary English. The goal was presumably to complement the more literal RSV with an idiomatic version. A general conference was held in October 1946, with representatives from Anglican, Presbyterian, Baptist, Methodist, Congregational, and other churches in Great Britain. The project was approved and C. H. Dodd, a leading British biblical scholar, was chosen to oversee the work. The New Testament was published in 1961 and the whole Bible, with Apocrypha, in 1970.

The preface, written by Dodd, notes that "the present translators were enjoined to replace Greek constructions and idioms by those of contemporary English ... We have conceived our task to be that of understanding the original as precisely as we could (using all available aids), and then saying again in our own native idiom what we believed the author to be saying in his." The NEB thus has the distinction of being the first church-approved version to break with the KJV tradition. The NEB was widely praised for its accuracy and fine literary style (C. S. Lewis was one of its stylists). Four million copies of the New Testament were sold in the first year. As noted previously, however, it has also been criticized for certain idiosyncrasies, including a literary style common to British academics.

Revised English Bible (1989). Two years after the publication of the NEB, a committee was formed to assess and critique the text. The eventual result was the REB, a major revision published in 1989. The "thees" and "thous" used for prayer in the NEB are removed and the somewhat colloquial style is revised. Certain idiosyncratic readings have been taken out and greater consistency is achieved. For example, the Greek word *ekklēsia* was rendered a variety of ways in the NEB: "church," "congregation," "meeting," "community." The REB more consistently uses "church." The REB also introduced a moderate use of gender inclusive language.

Jerusalem Bible (1966). Three Roman Catholic versions lie somewhere near the center of the translation spectrum (JB, NJB, NAB). The Jerusalem Bible arose in part as a result of an encyclical issued by Pope Pius XII in 1943 declaring that the original Hebrew and Greek text of Scripture had greater authority than ancient or modern versions. Prior to this, Roman Catholic versions were translated from the Latin Vulgate. In response to the encyclical, a group of Dominican scholars at the École Biblique in Jerusalem translated the Bible into French, the *Bible de Jérusalem*, which was published in 1956. This version was widely acclaimed for its accuracy and literary qualities, and an English edition was produced in 1966.

Although inspired by the French version, the JB was mostly translated from the original Greek and Hebrew. The JB is more idiomatic than the NAB, another Roman Catholic version (see below). One distinction of the JB is its rendering of the divine name (the Tetragrammaton, $YHWH$) as "Yahweh" rather than as the traditional "LORD."

New Jerusalem Bible (1985). When a new edition of the *Bible de Jérusalem*, the predecessor of the JB, was published in 1973, the decision was made to update the JB. Among other changes, the NJB introduced moderate use of gender inclusive language. The NJB is slightly more literal than its predecessor (JB) but somewhat freer than the NAB (see below). Like the JB, the NJB translates the Tetragrammaton as "Yahweh." For the traditional "LORD of hosts," the NJB has "Yahweh Sabaoth." Curiously, when the Hebrew idiom "son of man" means "human being," the NJB sometimes translates it with the evocative "child of Adam" (Num. 23:19; Ps. 8:4; Heb. 2:6).

New American Bible (1970; rev. 1991). The NAB is another Roman Catholic version that, like the JB, arose as a result of the 1943 encyclical of Pope Pius XII approving the authority of Bible versions translated directly from Hebrew and Greek texts. The New Testament of the NAB was originally based on the Confraternity Version of 1941 but was revised following the Hebrew and Greek. The complete NAB was released in 1970. It is more literal than the JB but more idiomatic than formal equivalent versions. The NAB sought to be more ecumenical than previous Catholic versions, and five of the fifteen members of its committee were Protestants. In 1986 a revised edition of the New Testament introduced, among other changes, the moderate use of gender inclusive language. In 1991 a revised edition of the Psalms did the same.

Tanakh (1985). The Jewish Publication Society's *The Holy Scriptures according to the Masoretic Text* (1917) was the standard Jewish version for most of the twentieth century. By the middle of the century, however, a more contemporary version was deemed necessary, and the JPS authorized a new translation. The result was the *Tanakh*, or New Jewish Version, published in stages (Torah, 1962; Prophets, 1978; Writings, 1982) and released as a whole in 1985. *Tanakh* is an acronym for the three sections of the Hebrew Bible (i.e., the Christian Old Testament): *Torah* (Law), *Nevi'im* (Prophets), and *Kethuvim* (Writings). The *Tanakh* is a well-respected version that utilizes the best of Jewish scholarship. It is a mediating version that steers a middle course between formal and functional equivalence.

Functional Equivalent Versions

The Living Bible (1971). Although more free than most functional equivalent versions, the Living Bible receives pride-of-place in this category, since it was the first idiomatic version to gain widespread acceptance. The LB was produced by Kenneth Taylor (d. 2005), who began rephrasing portions of the Bible in simplified English for his ten children for use during family devotions. In 1962 Taylor published *Living Letters*, a paraphrase of the New Testament letters. Other volumes followed. The full New Testament was published in 1966 and the whole Bible in 1971. Its lively, dynamic style made the LB extremely popular, especially among young people. Its endorsement and distribution by the Billy Graham Evangelistic Association also added greatly to its success. Tyndale House Publishers, the company Taylor formed to publish the work, has sold more than forty million copies.

As noted in chapter 2, the LB is a true "paraphrase," meaning a simplification and expansion of another English version. Taylor took the very literal ASV and simplified it into everyday language. The strength of this translation is its ability to communicate the message of the Bible in clear, fresh, and vivid ways to the readers. Its weakness, as we have seen, is a tendency to focus too much on contemporary relevance and not enough on original meaning.

The New Living Translation (1996; rev. 2004). The NLT is a major revision of the Living Bible. While the LB was the work of a single translator, with some translation consultants, the NLT is a committee work involving eighty-seven evangelical scholars from various denominations. While the original LB was a paraphrase, the NLT is a functional equivalent translation that seeks the closest natural equivalent in the receptor language. The goal, according to its preface, is to have "the same impact on the modern readers as the original had on its own audience."

The intentional shift from paraphrase to functional equivalence is evident in a verse like John 1:1. Whereas the LB read, "Before anything else existed, there was Christ," the NLT (1996) retains both the allusion to Genesis 1:1 and the Christological title "the Word": "In the beginning the Word already existed." A revised edition of the NLT was released in 2004. The NLT, like all recent functional equivalent versions, utilizes gender accurate language. In general it is a clear, accurate, and reliable translation.

Good News Translation (*Today's English Version*; *Good News Bible*; 1976; rev. 1992). The GNT/TEV/GNB was the first English version intentionally to adopt dynamic equivalence (= functional equivalence), the meaning-based translation principles developed by Eugene Nida and others involved in international Bible translation. The New Testament of the TEV, published as *Good News for Modern Man*, was translated by Robert Bratcher in consultation with a committee appointed by the American Bible Society (1966). The Old Testament was subsequently produced by a team of translators, and the whole Bible was published in 1976 under the title Good News Bible (GNB). The version has recently been renamed the Good News Translation (GNT).

The GNT is a clear, readable, and generally accurate version, which paved the way for other meaning-based versions. It has sometimes been criticized for oversimplifying the text and for imposing a uniform pedantic style on the highly diverse styles and genres of Scripture. A revised edition was introduced in 1992, which updated the translation generally and incorporated a moderate use of gender inclusive language.

Contemporary English Version (1995). The CEV arose from a series of studies conducted by translator and linguist Barclay Newman on how English is read and heard. These studies resulted in several idiomatic translations on individual biblical books, including *Luke Tells the Good News about Jesus* (1987) and *Good News Travels Fast — The Acts of the Apostles* (1988). The entire New Testament was released in 1991 and the whole Bible in 1995. Like the GNT, the CEV is a functional equivalent version intended to apply consistently the meaning-based principles developed by international translators. Like the GNT, it was produced under the auspices of the American Bible Society.

The CEV's strength is clarity and natural, idiomatic English. Its weakness may be a tendency to sacrifice precision for clarity. Traditional theological terms are replaced with natural, everyday language. While the TNIV translates Ephesians 2:8a, "For it is by grace you have been saved, through faith," the CEV reads, "You were saved by faith in God, who treats us much better than we deserve." The CEV preface identifies itself not as a replacement of other versions, but as "a *companion*—the *mission* arm—of traditional translations," which seeks to cross cultural boundaries that other versions do not. Recognizing that many people hear the Bible more than they read it, particular attention is given to the clarity of the text when read aloud. Like other meaning-based versions, the CEV uses gender inclusive language.

New Century Version and *International Children's Bible* (1986). The NCV and the ICB arose as revisions of a Bible originally designed for the deaf, produced by the World Translation Center of Fort Worth, Texas. The whole Bible was published in 1986 under two titles, the ICB for children and the NCV for more general readers. In 1991 the NCV was revised for a slightly higher reading level. Both versions are now published by Thomas Nelson.

The NCV is a functional equivalent version guided by two basic premises, faithfulness to the original text and clarity so that anyone can read and understand the Bible (NCV preface). Clarity is achieved especially through vocabulary selection based on *The Living Word Vocabulary*, the standard used by the editors of *The World Book Encyclopedia*. Difficult words are replaced with more easily understood terms: "justify" becomes "make right"; "genealogy" becomes "family history." Figures of speech and idiomatic expressions are clarified. The NCV has achieved marketing success especially through the publication of Nelson's "Bible-zines," glossy magazines with the text surrounded by pictures and articles geared for teens and young adults.

God's Word (1995). GW was produced by God's Word to the Nations Bible Society in Cleveland, Ohio, an organization associated with the Missouri Synod of the Lutheran Church. In its preface the version claims to be using neither formal equivalence nor functional equivalence, but rather "closest natural equivalence"—a translation policy that avoids the awkwardness of literal versions and the purported loss of meaning of idiomatic ones. Despite this attempt to distinguish itself from other versions, GW clearly fits into the genre of functional equivalent versions like the NLT, GNT, CEV, and NCV. The version is generally accurate and readable, comparable to other functional equivalent versions in quality and style.

New International reader's Version (1996). We have already noted the International Children's Bible, a version of the NCV. Another important children's version is the New International reader's Version (NIrV; 1996), a simplified English version based on the NIV. It is designed for children, adults with lower reading skills, and those for whom English is a second language. Simplicity and ease of understanding are its hallmarks. Like the NIV, the NIrV is copyrighted by the International Bible Society (IBS) and published by Zondervan. The IBS website for the NIrV summarizes its purpose:

> The NIrV was designed to make the Bible clear and understandable to early readers and can be read by a typical fourth grader. For this reason, it is also of value to the millions for whom English is a second language. It intends to be distinguished by five fundamental characteristics—readability, understandability, compatibility with the NIV, reliability, and trustworthiness. It serves as a natural stepping-stone to the NIV when the time is right.

The Message (2002). We have already discussed The Message in some detail in chapter 2. This popular version was translated by Eugene Peterson, with various scholars serving as translation consultants. The New Testament appeared in 1993 and the whole Bible in 2002. Its lively and engaging language has struck a chord with many readers—much like the Living Bible in the 1960s and 1970s—and has made the text a popular supplement to traditional versions. Peterson's goal was to convert the tone, rhythm, and ideas of the Bible into the way people think and speak today. The Message is a response-oriented Bible, seeking vivid relevance more than historical precision.

Some Recommendations

Throughout this book we have encouraged the use of multiple versions from across the translation spectrum. No translation is perfect and all provide helpful insights into the meaning of the text. We would recommend consulting any of the twenty-five versions we have surveyed above. If we had to choose a few from each category, below are our recommendations.

The NRSV is perhaps the most reliable of the formal equivalent versions and is well respected among biblical scholars. The NASB, NASU is the most consistently literal and so provides the most direct access to the form and structure of the Hebrew and Greek. The ESV is an improvement over the RSV, especially in light of its greater use of gender accurate language (see p. 97 above).

For a mediating version, which we believe to be the best general purpose Bible, the TNIV is perhaps your best choice. Like its predecessor, the NIV, it is a committee translation that draws on the best of evangelical scholarship. It improves on the NIV both in its gender accuracy and its exegetical precision. In the interest of full disclosure, we should remind readers that both authors serve on its translation committee (though we have also been involved with other versions). The NET and NAB are also excellent and reliable versions. Like the TNIV, both are committee works representing a high level of biblical scholarship. The additional notes in the NET are particularly helpful for those doing detailed study. The NAB represents the best of Roman Catholic scholarship.

Functional equivalent versions are excellent reading Bibles, especially when reading entire books in one setting. By using natural and idiomatic English, they seek to make the text sound as clear and natural to modern readers as it sounded to the original readers. Functional equivalent versions are also helpful for detailed study, and especially as a complement to Hebrew and Greek study. This is because while literal versions tend to simply reproduce Hebrew and Greek grammatical forms, functional equivalent versions go further and clarify the "functional" relationships between phrases and clauses. In this way they answer the syntactical and exegetical questions that advanced students are asking about the text.

There are many good choices among the functional equivalent versions. The NLT, especially in its 2004 revision, is accurate, clear, and readable. Like the TNIV and the NET, it is a committee work with a high level of scholarship behind its translation. The NCV, GW, CEV, and GNT (TEV/GNB) are also good choices. The Message can provide fresh insights into the text and its application, but should always be used with other more historically accurate versions.

Given such a rich store of available options, we hope by this book to bring some measure of help to the contemporary English reader, both in understanding the options and in selecting a primary Bible of use. But whatever else, reading *about* translations is not the same as reading the Bible itself. So we conclude by urging the reader, in the words heard by Augustine that led to his moment of conversion, "*Tolle lege.*" "Take up and read!"

For Further Reading

Comfort, Philip W. *Essential Guide to Bible Versions.* Wheaton, IL: Tyndale, 2000.

Dewey, David. *A User's Guide to Bible Translations: Making the Most of Different Versions.* Downers Grove, IL: InterVarsity Press, 2004.

Kubo, Sakae, and Walter Specht. *So Many Versions? Twentieth-Century English Versions of the Bible.* Grand Rapids: Zondervan, 1983.

Lewis, Jack P. *The English Bible from the KJV to the NIV: A History and Evaluation.* 2nd ed. Grand Rapids: Baker, 1991.

Glossary

Critical text. Greek text achieved by using the methods of textual criticism to identify and eliminate copyist errors. The standard critical editions of the Greek New Testament are the Nestle-Aland 27th edition (NA^{27}) and the United Bible Societies' 4th edition (UBS^4).

Dead metaphor. A metaphor that has lost its concrete image in the minds of readers, who move directly to the abstract meaning. "That's just sour grapes" is a dead metaphor in most contexts, since few readers would think of grapes when they heard it.

Diaspora. A word meaning "dispersion" and referring to Jews living outside of Palestine. Most Diaspora Jews of the first century spoke Greek.

Dynamic equivalence. An older name for *functional equivalence*, coined by Eugene Nida.

External (textual) evidence. Evidence that is used to evaluate the value of a manuscript for discerning the original text of Scripture. External evidence includes the age of a manuscript, its "family" identification, and the geographical distribution of its readings.

Formal equivalence. A translation philosophy, also known as "literal" or "word-for-word" translation, that seeks to retain the *form* of the Hebrew or Greek as much as possible.

Functional equivalence. A translation philosophy, also known as idiomatic or meaning-based translation (and formerly known as dynamic equivalence), that seeks to reproduce the *meaning* of the text in good idiomatic (natural) English, regardless of the form.

Gender accurate language. Language that intentionally clarifies or specifies whether references are to males only or to both males and females.

Gender inclusive language. A synonym for "gender accurate" language; language that intentionally clarifies or specifies whether references are to males only or to both males and females.

Generic language. Language that refers generally to people, both males and females. The English word "men" has traditionally been used as a generic term for both men and women.

Idiomatic translation. See *functional equivalence.*

Internal (textual) evidence. Evidence that is used to evaluate the value of individual variants (or readings) within the textual tradition of the Hebrew Old Testament and the Greek New Testament. Internal evidence seeks to discern the tendencies of authors and copyists and so to work backward to determine the original text of Scripture.

Lexeme. A fundamental unit of the vocabulary of a language. A lexeme is the form of the word you would look up in a dictionary. For example, "make" is one lexeme, but it takes various forms in different contexts (make, makes, made, making, etc.).

Lexical concordance. The translation goal of trying consistently to use the same word in the receptor language (e.g., English) for a particular word in the source language (e.g., Hebrew or Greek).

Lexical semantics. The study of words and their meanings.

"Literal" translation. See *formal equivalence.*

Live metaphor. A metaphor in which the implicit comparison continues to be evoked in the mind of readers. "God is a rock" is a live metaphor since the image of a rock remains in the mind of the reader. "He's rock solid" is (probably) a dead metaphor since the reader will immediately move to the meaning "He's dependable" without considering the characteristics of a rock.

Majority Text. The Greek text of the New Testament achieved by following the readings of the majority of manuscripts; also known as the Byzantine text. Since the majority of manuscripts are late, copied between AD 1000 and 1540, the Majority Text is generally viewed as inferior to the text found in the Critical Text, which represents the readings of earlier manuscripts.

Manuscript. A hand-copied document. Textual critics study the manuscripts of the Hebrew Old Testament and Greek New Testament to determine the original text of Scripture.

Masoretic Text. The "standard" Hebrew text named after the Jewish scribes known as the Masoretes, who meticulously copied it. The standard edition used in colleges, universities, and seminaries is the *Biblia Hebraica Stuttgartensia* (5th edition).

Mediating version. A translation that occupies the middle ground between formal and functional equivalence.

Metaphor. A figure of speech that uses one thing to describe something else by way of comparison. "God is a rock" is a metaphor. See also *simile, dead metaphor, live metaphor.*

Metonymy. A figure of speech where one thing is used for something related to it (e.g., "The pen is mightier than the sword").

Paraphrase. Used in different, sometimes contradictory, ways: (1) *negatively*: of an overly free translation; (2) *neutrally*: of saying the same thing using different words, for the sake of clarity or simplicity; (3) *technically in linguistics*: rewriting or restating a message in the *same* language, in contrast to translation, which is rewriting or restating a message in a *different* language.

Receptor language. The language into which a translation is made; also known as the target language.

Register. Type or level of language used in a particular social situation or when communicating with a particular set of people. Language with a "higher register" is directed toward those with a larger vocabulary and greater competence in that language.

Septuagint. The Greek translation of the Hebrew Scriptures, produced beginning in the third century BC. The word means "seventy" and is named after the legend that seventy (or seventy-two) Hebrew scholars produced it. It is abbreviated "LXX," the Roman numeral for "seventy."

Simile. A figure of speech comparing one thing to another, especially in a phrase containing the word "like" or "as" (e.g., "We are all like sheep"). See also *metaphor.*

Source language. The language of the text being translated; also known as the original or donor language. See also *receptor language.*

Synecdoche. A figure of speech where a part of something is used for the whole, or vice versa. "He owns a nice set of wheels" (part for whole); "California just passed a new law" (whole for part).

Syntactic correspondence. Translation goal that seeks to reproduce the grammar or syntax of the original text as closely as possible.

Textual criticism. The science and art of studying the Hebrew and Greek manuscripts of the Bible to determine the original words of Scripture.

Textus Receptus. The edition of the Greek New Testament used to translate the King James Version. The Textus Receptus was based on only a few late Greek manuscripts and so is not as reliable as modern critical editions of the Greek New Testament.

Transculturation. Reformulating the historical meaning of the text to fit a new cultural situation. Transculturation goes beyond "translation," which reproduces the *same historical* meaning in a different language. Clarence Jordan's *Cotton Patch Version* is an extreme form of transculturation.

Transliteration. The practice of spelling out the form of a word in one language with the letters of another language. For example, *abba* is an English transliteration of an Aramaic word meaning "father." "Father" is a translation; *abba* is a transliteration.

Word-for-word translation. See *formal equivalence*.

Notes

Chapter 2: The Meaning and Task of Translation

1. Martin Luther, *Luther's Works* (Philadelphia: Muhlenberg, 1960), 35:193.
2. See http://www.navpress.com/BibleProducts/HistoryAndFaqs/#05.
3. Robert Young, "Preface to the Revised Edition" (no page number; italics and capitals in original). This book has been published by a variety of publishers since the mid-1800s.
4. J. B. Phillips, *Letters to Young Churches* (New York: MacMillan, 1947), xii.

Chapter 3: Translating Words

1. For these and many other examples, see Richard Lederer, *Crazy English: The Ultimate Joy Ride through Our Language* (New York: Pocket Books, 1989), 74–75.
2. Ibid., excerpts from chap. 1.

Chapter 4: Translating Figurative Language: Idioms, Metaphors, and Poetry

1. Gordon D. Fee and Douglas Stuart, *How to Read the Bible for All Its Worth*, 3rd ed. (Grand Rapids: Zondervan, 2003), 206–8.

Chapter 7: Gender and Translation

1. William Lane, *Hebrews* (Word Biblical Commentary; Waco, TX: Word, 1991), 1:47–48.

Notes

Chapter 2: The Meaning and Task of Translation

Chapter 3: Translating Words

Chapter 4: Translating Figurative Language: Idioms, Metaphors, and Poetry

Chapter 7: Gender and Translation

Index

Share Your Thoughts

With the Author: Your comments will be forwarded to the author when you send them to *zauthor@zondervan.com*.

With Zondervan: Submit your review of this book by writing to *zreview@zondervan.com*.

Free Online Resources at
www.zondervan.com

Zondervan AuthorTracker: Be notified whenever your favorite authors publish new books, go on tour, or post an update about what's happening in their lives at www.zondervan.com/authortracker.

Daily Bible Verses and Devotions: Enrich your life with daily Bible verses or devotions that help you start every morning focused on God. Visit www.zondervan.com/newsletters.

Free Email Publications: Sign up for newsletters on Christian living, academic resources, church ministry, fiction, children's resources, and more. Visit www.zondervan.com/newsletters.

Zondervan Bible Search: Find and compare Bible passages in a variety of translations at www.zondervanbiblesearch.com.

Other Benefits: Register to receive online benefits like coupons and special offers, or to participate in research.

ZONDERVAN.com/
AUTHORTRACKER
follow your favorite authors